DEVELOPMENTS IN ISRAELI PUBLIC ADMINISTRATION

ISRAELI HISTORY, POLITICS AND SOCIETY
Series Editor: Efraim Karsh, King's College London
ISSN: 1368-4795

This series provides a multidisciplinary examination of all aspects of Israeli history, politics and society, and serves as a means of communication between the various communities interested in Israel: academics, policy-makers, practitioners, journalists and the informed public.

1. *Peace in the Middle East: The Challenge for Israel,* edited by Efraim Karsh.

2. *The Shaping of Israeli Identity: Myth, Memory and Trauma,* edited by Robert Wistrich and David Ohana.

3. *Between War and Peace: Dilemmas of Israeli Security,* edited by Efraim Karsh.

4. *U.S.-Israeli Relations at the Crossroads,* edited by Gabriel Sheffer.

5. *Revisiting the Yom Kippur War,* edited by P. R. Kumaraswamy.

6. *Israel: The Dynamics of Change and Continuity,* edited by David Levi-Faur, Gabriel Sheffer and David Vogel.

7. *In Search of Identity: Jewish Aspects in Israeli Culture,* edited by Dan Urian and Efraim Karsh.

8. *Israel at the Polls, 1996,* edited by Daniel J. Elazar and Shmuel Sandler.

9. *From Rabin to Netanyahu: Israel's Troubled Agenda,* edited by Efraim Karsh.

10. *Fabricating Israeli History: The 'New Historians',* second revised edition, by Efraim Karsh.

11. *Divided Against Zion: Anti-Zionist Opposition in Britain to a Jewish State in Palestine, 1945-1948,* by Rory Miller.

12. *Peacemaking in a Divided Society: Israel After Rabin,* edited by Sasson Sofer.

13. *A Twenty-Year Retrospective of Egyptian-Israeli Relations: Peace in Spite of Everything,* by Ephraim Dowek.

14. *Global Politics: Essays in Honour of David Vital,* edited by Abraham Ben-Zvi and Aharon Klieman.

15. *Parties, Elections and Cleavages; Israel in Comparative and Theoretical Perspective,* edited by Reuven Y. Hazan and Moshe Maor.

16. *Israel at the Polls 1999,* edited by Daniel J. Elazar and M. Ben Mollov.

17. *Public Policy in Israel,* edited by David Nachmias and Gila Menahem.

18. *Developments in Israeli Public Administration,* edited by Moshe Maor.

Israel: The First Hundred Years (Mini Series), edited by Efraim Karsh.

1. *Israel's Transition from Community to State,* edited by Efraim Karsh.

2. *From War to Peace?* edited by Efraim Karsh.

3. *Politics and Society Since 1948,* edited by Efraim Karsh.

4. *Israel in the International Arena,* edited by Efraim Karsh.

DEVELOPMENTS IN ISRAELI PUBLIC ADMINISTRATION

Edited by
Moshe Maor

Foreword by
Yehezkel Dror

Routledge
Taylor & Francis Group

LONDON AND NEW YORK

First published 2002 by Frank Cass publishers

2 Park Square, Milton Park, Abingdon, Oxfordshire OX14 4RN
605 Third Avenue, New York, NY 10017

Routledge is an imprint of the Taylor & Francis Group, an informa business

First issued in paperback 2020

British Library Cataloguing in Publication Data

Developments in Israeli public administration. – (Israeli
history, politics and society ; v. 18)
1.Public administration – Israel 2.Israel – Politics and
government
I.Maor, Moshe
351.5'694

ISBN 978-0-7146-5302-0 (cloth)
ISBN 978-0-7146-8263-1 (pbk)
ISSN 1368-4795

Library of Congress Cataloging-in-Publication Data

Developments in Israeli public administration / edited by Moshe Maor.
  p. cm. — (Israeli history, politics, and society, ISSN
1368-4795 ; 18)
"This group of studies first appeared as 'Developments in Israeli Public
Administration', a special issue of Israel Affairs, Vol.8, No.4 (Summer,
2002)."
Includes bibliographical references and index.
  ISBN 0-7146-5302-0 (hardback) — ISBN 0-7146-8263-2 (pbk.)
  1. Public administration—Israel. I. Maor, Moshe. II. Israel affairs.
Special issue. III. Series.
  JQ1830.A58 D475 2002
  351.5694—dc21
                    2002004670

This group of studies first appeared as 'Developments in Israeli Public Administration',
a special issue of *Israel Affairs*, Vol.8, No.4 (Summer 2002),

Contents

Foreword

YEHEZKEL DROR

It is hard to imagine more compact and dense a social science laboratory than the State of Israel. Take a small area, throw into it waves of diverse immigrants, add rapid transitions between wars and peace, divide the population between various belief systems, introduce complex links with external groups and global cultures, subject the society to rapid transformations – and you have what is both the State of Israel and a unique setting for studying complex processes in a small enough area to be comprehensible as a whole.

Regretfully, however much Israeli and other social scientists[1] research the shifting realities of Israel, this is an underutilized laboratory. Thus, good books on Israeli governance are very scarce, even in Hebrew. All the more welcome is this collection, which explores some main aspects of the public administration of Israel in ways providing novel insights and comparative material for the study of public administration as an academic discipline and an applied profession.

To help to understand fully the various chapters and draw theoretical and comparative conclusions, some broader contextual perspectives may be useful. Let me suggest seven that may help to locate the various discussed subjects within a systemic view:

1. Israel is the most ideological of all contemporary democracies

While all states are similar in some respects and unique in others, Israel is radically unique among democracies in having a dominant ideology, namely Zionism. Thus, it should be born in mind that it was Zionism which produced the population basis of Israel, by encouraging immigration, this being a unique feature in comparison to other state-building ideologies.

However diluted and controversial, the vast majority of the Jewish population of Israel adheres to Zionism in the sense of wishing Israel to be a Jewish-Zionist state while also being a democracy. This imposes a double set of tasks on the government of Israel and its public administration, namely to engage in building the state and assuring its Jewish-Zionist future, while also serving the desires and needs of the present populations, including the non-Jewish minorities. The tensions between those two sets of tasks serve to explain some of the features of Israel's public administration within its governmental and political environments.

2. Social architecture is widely accepted as a governmental task

Let me further elaborate the aforementioned feature by emphasizing the social architecture tasks of the government, going far beyond 'welfare state' models. Thus, in addition to immigration and its integration, the dispersal of populations, education that strengthens commitment to Jewish-Zionist values, and the integration of Israel with the Jewish People as a whole are among the social architecture tasks accepted by the vast majority of senior politicians, in addition to all the usual functions of government.

This further complicates the self-image and mission conceptions of the civil service, between serving the public and participating in societal value-driven architecture.

3. Government is in charge of critical future-weaving choices and actions

There is no other democracy where the government is faced by choices with the very survival of the state and society at stake. Other democracies do confront choices with radical implications for the future, such as joining the European Community and joining the European currency agreement. However, these are not matters of survival, as are at stake in the political and security choices of Israel, such as the Palestinian issue and coping with a possible Iranian nuclear threat.

Israeli decision-makers are well aware of the critical nature of their choices as well as their inherent nature as 'fuzzy gambles'.[2] Little wonder that other less fateful issues are neglected, including reforming public administration.

4. Scarcity of strategic thinking

It is easy to argue that the very nature of the ideological commitments and realpolitical problems of Israel require top quality long-term strategic thinking. In some domains, especially in security matters, there are professional staffs engaging in such thinking, augmented by the National Security Council established in 1999.[3] Another interesting innovation is the establishment in 2002 of a 'Commissioner of Future Generations' in the Israeli Parliament, who has the authority to delay legislation until longer-term implications are examined.[4] However, nearly all ministries lack strategic staff units, and the Prime Minister's Office itself has very few, with the exception of the new National Security Council, the impact of which on crucial choices is as yet unclear.

Many explanations can be offered for the weaknesses of long-term strategic thinking, such as an overload of current issues and rapid shifts in situations. But the basic reasons are probably rapid turnover of ministers; lack of policy professionalism in the senior civil service; oscillation between situations which are 'good' and therefore seem not to require long-term strategic thinking and situations which are 'bad' and leave no mental resources available for such thinking; and a tradition of relying on 'doing' and improvisation.

5. Political fragmentation

If one asks what is the single most important trend in Israeli politics it is fragmentation. Israel has always had coalition governments, but until 1977 there was a dominant party providing much stability and continuity, while increasingly losing touch with social realities. This has changed totally, with Israeli politics being characterized not only by many parties, none of which is dominant, but also by multiple political cultures – such as orthodox religious, Arab and some Jewish ethnic ones.

The results include weak governmental coalitions preventing coordination, increasing political domination of the civil service, more intense personal and party political competition, various efforts to change the electoral systems which failed and were reversed, and other features of a growing 'incapacity to govern',[5] shared in part with other democracies – such as image marketing taking over from programmatic party politics.

6. No professional civil service elite compensating for weaknesses of the political system

Given the transitional crisis of Israeli politics while it is faced with crucial and very divisive choices, one could expect a coherent professional civil service to compensate for the weaknesses of the political system, as happened in some sense during the French Third Republic. But Israel has no professional civil service elite. There are many professional civil servants, but they do not operate as a governmental strata enjoying much autonomy. Rather, they are divided between the ministries without much interaction and function under the sway of the ministers without real professional autonomy.

7. Political structures, processes and cultures inhibit administrative reforms

Israel is one of the few advanced societies which has not had a substantive administrative reform since the establishment of the state in 1948. There was one reform commission that proposed radical changes in the civil service and the machinery of government, but nothing was done even though the Cabinet twice approved the recommendations. Following a short visit to the UK, an effort was made to introduce New Public Management reforms (as described in one of the chapters), again without any impact.

Of course, many changes were made to the civil service, some quite useful. But the basic principles of the civil service are increasingly obsolete, further increasing incapacities to govern. However, political interest and the will to improve public administration do not exist.

Let me conclude these perspectives by posing an encompassing riddle to which I have no complete answer, even though I have spent a lifetime studying Israeli government and fulfilling senior positions within it. It is easy to explain incapacities to govern when governments are corrupt, politicians lack commitment to national goals and civil servants are unqualified. However, these failings are not prevalent in Israel. When talking individually with most politicians and senior civil servants, the vast majority are intelligent, committed, personally honest and often quite knowledgeable. But, working as a collective in government, overall performance is often, though certainly not always, very disappointing. Therefore, governmental structures and culture somehow produce in the aggregate much less than one would expect from the quality of its components. Instead of a synergistic aggregation function, interactions are somehow 'negative' and depress the outputs of the governance system as a whole.

This is just a sub-riddle in the larger question: how Israel is so successful in many domains despite its pronounced weaknesses of governments and public administration. This is an issue with far-reaching theoretical and applied implications on the causes of societal rise and decline, on evaluating results and on what really is important in the operations of governments. These riddles cannot be taken up here, but the careful reader with find in the chapters of this collection some insights relevant to such broader issues, in addition to learning much about some fascinating specifics of public administration in Israel, interesting in themselves and useful mosaics for a better comparative, theoretical and practical understanding of governance and public administration.

NOTES

1. Studying Israel in depth requires good knowledge of Hebrew, available material in English, however proliferating, being inadequate – even if supplemented by interviews – for acquiring a good understanding of very complex and rapidly changing structures and processes.
2. For a discussion of this concept and its implications, see Yehezkel Dror, *The Capacity to Govern: A Report to the Club of Rome*, London: Frank Cass, 2001, ch.15.
3. In substance, this is a National Security Staff, not a 'Council' composed of top decision-makers as in the United States.
4. It will take a couple of years to see how this interesting innovation will work out. So far, the Parliament has not provided the Commissioner with the minimum professional staff essential for seriously fulfilling his functions.
5. For detailed discussion and improvement proposals, see Dror, *The Capacity to Govern*.

Introduction

MOSHE MAOR

For much of the time since the Israeli bureaucracy was created, it was a classic example of centralized organization in which politicians at the apex sought to control the behaviour of the staff at the periphery through a combination of central planning and national directives.[1] The weakness of this command and control system led to some developments in both the structure of the bureaucracy and the way it works. These developments will be analysed in this volume, with special concern for decision-making and -makers. The study of decision-making in bureaucracies has been a central concern of social scientists in the last few decades; thus it has been addressed in theoretical terms as well as in analytical historical descriptions.[2] The articles presented here revolve around the latter approach in order to gauge the systemic faults faced by Israeli political executives trying to introduce administrative reforms.[3]

The central questions faced by Israeli political executives nowadays are twofold. Are bureaucratic structures the problem or the solution? Are civil servants the problem or the solution? Whether command and control mechanisms ('first way') have given way to market forces ('second way'), or to a variety of mechanisms used according to circumstances ('third way') is yet to be seen. Perhaps what is more important at this stage is the direction of developments in the Israeli administrative system and the derived consequence in terms of the answer to the aforementioned central questions.

HISTORICAL BACKGROUND

The Israeli bureaucracy has been on the defensive ever since the politics of restraint began. During the late 1980s, a revolt against the Israeli bureaucracy manifested itself by expenditure reduction and measures to contain the public purse, followed during the mid-1990s by efforts of political executives to roll back the state through some combination of privatization, contracting out, deregulation and programme termination. On numerous occasions, bureaucracy-bashing accompanied the politics of restraint. The rise in political appointments and the increase in political executives blaming senior officials for overdoing expenditure reductions made relations between politicians and civil servants sour, and public service morale plummeted. However, no concerted attempt to perform radical surgery on the Israeli administrative system was recorded.

During 1999, two delegations comprising director generals of government ministries undertook study visits to the UK to learn more from the British model of reforms. In early January 2000, another delegation comprised of the minister responsible for public administration reform, the director general of the Prime Minister's Office and senior civil servants, visited the UK for the same purpose. In February 2000, the Prime Minister Conference on Public Sector Reforms took place, and consequently, the Public–Professional Committee for New Public Management was appointed 'to examine the structure of the public sector and accommodate its structural and organizational bases, as well as its behavioural modes, to the needs and tasks with which it is, and will be, confronted'.[4] With the resignation of Ehud Barak, this committee was abolished.

An important contextual factor is that such initiatives are taking place in an increasingly turbulent and uncertain international environment. This is associated with the failure of the peace process and the start of the second *intifada*, as well as with the spread of corporate capitalism, globalization and the participation of Israel in international systems of cooperation such as the World Trade Organization. These sets of environmental changes are being accompanied and fuelled by a technological revolution, based on advanced computer systems, which is transforming the means of communication across the world, concentrating space and time and creating an information and knowledge explosion.

THE OPTIONS FOR REFORMS

A gradual move away from the traditional precepts of Weberian bureaucracy seems therefore to be on its way. The question is, towards what? Although speculation is not a scholar's profession, it seems reasonable to expect, as always in the Israeli context, that the answer is most likely to be multifaceted, that is, different parts of the Israeli public administration will move in different directions. An elaboration of the optional policies for the public sector is illuminating especially if done in the light of the variety of assumptions on the part of politicians about the motivations of civil servants.

Some ministerial departments may remain under the ambit of the Weberian model. The view of political executives regarding the motivation of public servants in these departments rests on the following core assumption: that those at the centre of organizations have the task of making sure that their objectives are carried through. This is accomplished by making clear what those objectives are and seeing that they are implemented at the lower levels. Similarly there is an understanding that those at the top of the organization know better than those at the bottom what need be done. It follows from these two assumptions that discretion on the part of civil servants should be minimized through central control and supervision of performance in the organization.

Other ministries may follow the New Public Management (NPM) model. Some academics have laid out a series of principles guiding the changes sought in the organization of government operations and personnel across Western democracies.[5] These changes can be summarized as follows: (1) from hierarchical to economic-based structures; (2) from regulative to economic-based processes; and (3) from legally based to economic-based values. These principles include an emphasis on management skills to complement policy skills; a shift from the use of input controls and bureaucratic procedures and rules to a reliance on quantifiable output measures and performance targets; the devolution of management control coupled with the development of reporting, monitoring and accountability strategies; a preference for the introduction of market forces in public service provision; a disaggregation of large bureaucratic structures into quasi-autonomous agencies, in particular, separating the commercial from non-commercial functions, and policy advice from policy implementation; the imitation of certain private sector management practices, such as the use of short-term labour contracts and the development of mission statements and performance agreements; a shift towards using monetary rather than non-monetary incentives; and an emphasis on cost-cutting, efficiency and cutback management.[6]

Here the assumption about the motivation of civil servants is that planning is likely to be less effective than competition in producing change. Proponents of this idea posit that public employees respond favourably to the incentive programme with which they are presented. If they can enhance the resources available to their organization through competition, they will do so. Likewise, if it is clear that the failure to compete successfully will result in closure, then their motivation to change their behaviour in order to survive is increased. This alternative policy towards public bureaucracy recognizes that there is a limit to how much control can be exercised by the centre over the periphery and as such chooses to empower staff to independent action more than controlling them.

Other ministerial departments may be moving towards a mix of mechanisms used according to circumstances. Such policies recognize the limits of central control and staff empowerment in public administration. Rather than rejecting them entirely though, they try to combine them in a complex melange of policy inputs. In addition to planning and competition, these policies make use of other tools such as innovative methods of inspection, regulation and the publication of information of comparative performance in the area of policy with which the organization is involved. What stems from this is the implicit understanding that human behaviour is motivated by complex factors and that this complexity was not taken into account by advocates of either the first or the second policy alternatives. If policy-makers are to be able to deliver on their objectives, therefore, they will have to employ a broader spectrum of instruments.

Given the evident diversity of activity in the Israeli bureaucracy, it may not be appropriate to think in terms of general prescriptions of how a type of reform should be applied. Some parts of the public sector can be expected to benefit greatly from the adoption of NPM reform, other parts of the public services may find some ideas more difficult to apply. In addition, a few factors may inhibit reform. The weakness of mechanisms for policy control, monitoring and evaluation; an administrative culture which is characterized by frequent infringements of moral integrity; and a relatively high level of politicization are all obstacles to reform. So far, the political solution of these problems, in the context where the assignment of blame for errors is a major occupation of opposition parties and of the media, has been greater intervention by political executives. This has ensured that discretionary authority within the administrative apparatus has been given mainly to those who meet the requisite tests of ardour for the goals and methods of the elected authorities.[7] It is precisely the resolution of this problem that the success of any reform is dependent on and will be judged upon. It is therefore crucial that recent developments of the Israeli public administration undertaken in the aforementioned context over the last ten years be described and analysed, so as to understand that experience, and to provide decision-makers who are about to undertake a concerted attempt to reform the public sector with guidance on what kind of reform may be successful and for which part of the public sector.

AN OVERVIEW OF THE VOLUME

The first article in this volume, written by Aharon Kfir, analyses the formation of the core bureaucracy in Israel, that is, the government departments. At the outset, the lack of research into the question of why the Israeli state bureaucracy took its current form is rather puzzling. The problem is both theoretically and instrumentally important for political scientists, sociologists and economists. In terms of theory the problem is related to the general question of state formation and organizational change within the state and its political structure. Instrumentally, the problem is related to the process by which the rationalization of the state bureaucracy was originally institutionalized in the country investigated.[8] Kfir's article falls under the latter umbrella.

In his article Kfir suggests that Israel's civil service, in general, and the structure of its government offices, in particular, have been fraught with problems ever since the state was established. The article examines the process that led to the creation of government offices during 1943 to 1948. Based on historical and institutional analysis, it shows that a great deal of thought was given to the structure of the government service. The outcome was a well-founded structure for government offices, well able to stand the test of modern administrative challenges. The distortions in the execution of this plan stemmed, and still stem, in the main, from non-compliance with the detailed original plans, owing mainly to political considerations. Since the establishment of the state there has been continuous criticism of the structure of government administration and there have been numerous proposals for change. Almost every one of these proposals was aimed at the elimination of three main shortcomings: curtailment of the number of government offices; reorganization of the functions of the various offices in order to maximize coordination; and development of directional planning and coordinated supervision of activities – all of which the earlier planning had tried to obviate in its proposals.

The contribution of Eva Etzioni-Halevy, which follows Kfir's article, focuses on developments in both the structure of the bureaucracy and the way it works. Etzioni-Halevy posits that the power of the state administration in Israel is considerable but not autonomous. Rather, the administrative elite is dependent on the political elite through political appointments and promotions in some major parts of the state bureaucracy. By virtue of this close but unequal connection, administrative power is linked to party politics and works in its service: senior bureaucrats have been instrumental in various forms of electoral manipulation. Over the years there have been changes and developments, but there has been no fundamental transformation of these arrangements. This creates severe problems for Israeli democracy. The electoral manipulation brought about by administrative politicization has not destroyed democracy. But it has not been negligible in determining electoral outcomes. Hence it has detracted from the quality of democracy in Israel.

Ira Sharkansky in his article probes how distinctive features of Israeli public administration reflect underlying traits of the nation's history, culture and geography. The concentration of people in part of the small state produces a dominant metropolitan region. The formal structure and procedures are those of a strong national government, and there is a high incidence of former technocrats in elected positions. The image is of a tightly run, professional state. However, the formal structure provides imperfect indications of how policy-making and programme implementation really operate. Other features of the political culture, along with the high incidence of intense problems, create a messy polity where coping rather than problem-solving prevails.

Robert Schwartz's thought-provoking article addresses the simply phrased, but highly troubling question: is Israel's government out of control? This article provides a snapshot of the state of administrative and financial control of government activities in Israel. Budgeting, evaluation and auditing mechanisms are examined in light of changes in international approaches and practice – post-bureaucratic control and the advent of the 'audit society'. There is no lack of control mechanisms, including a plethora of audit functions, but their implementation is weak. Bureaucratic procedural compliance dominates both budgeting and auditing practice at the expense of post-bureaucratic, results-based control. There is little parliamentary supervision. And budgeting, auditing and evaluation activities are weakly linked. Explanations of the sorry state of administrative control in Israel include: agenda overload; highly politicized coalition-type governments; and a cultural tendency of lack of thoroughness.

The following article, by Yoav Dotan, describes the general characteristics of the judicial system in Israel and its relationship with other institutions in Israeli society including the Israeli administrative system. It presents a model of society within which the courts (and, in particular, the Supreme Court) play a paramount political role by routinely intervening in the practices of public administration as well as in the business of other governmental and non-governmental institutions, and thereby bringing about a judicialization of society. The courts intervene in decision-making processes of political executives, and this widespread intervention brings about a process of adaptation to patterns of legal thinking and judicial decision-making by many other administrative institutions. Dotan calls this model of highly intensive judicial intervention 'judicial hyperactivism'.

In the next article, Moshe Maor asks the following question: if there is a choice of institutional designs for the regulation of public utilities, how can such a choice between, for example, a single- or a multiple-industry regulator be made? This question is addressed by focusing on the design of the Israeli Public Utility Authority – Electricity, with special attention to the ways it has interpreted the requirements set by law regarding accountability, transparency and procedural fairness. The premise underlying the analysis is that regulators need to satisfy values of accountability, transparency and procedural fairness if they are to receive the approval of all parties concerned. A failure to implement choices that reflect these values implies that, whatever the substantive merits of such decisions, the subsequent regulation is unlikely to be successful. Based on institutional and historical analysis, combined with interviews with public officials involved with the design of the electricity regulator, Maor's article analyses the formation of the Public Utilities Commission (PUC) with an emphasis on the prominence, or lack thereof, of the aforementioned values in the Electricity Market Law 1996 and the PUC experience gained so far. The analysis finds that a lack of balance exists between the great discretion enjoyed by the Authority over tariffs and standard-setting, on the one hand, and its weak transparency, accountability and procedural fairness, on the other. Maor recommends an urgent revision of the law. In addition, to avoid creating other regulatory agencies that will suffer from similar structural and procedural flaws, the paper recommends the design of accountable, transparent and procedurally fair, single-industry regulators.

The final article in the volume is the work of Asher Friedberg. The piece discusses the role of state and public audit entities in Israel in safeguarding ethics in the public service. It relates to ambiguities and complexities concerning the legal and content infrastructure in light of which the state comptroller examines ethical issues in the public service sector, and refers to approaches of state comptrollers, past and present, to ethical issues in this sector. The article analyses a series of events and findings that were defined by state comptrollers as infringements of moral integrity, trying to identify patterns of infringements and to trace actions taken to remedy these infringements. The article mentions activities of other public comptrollers (the Labour Federation and the Jewish Agency) to moral integrity issues. The article points to ethical aspects in the activities of the State Comptroller's Office itself, and concludes by emphasizing problems stemming from the discussion in the article.

In attempting to explain change and inertia in the Israeli public administration we perhaps need to look not only at generally exaggerated faults but also at its capacity for external and internal adaptability. Perhaps the dominant explanations of early 2000 may be less critical of the alleged inherent defects of the Israeli public administration, and more sensitive to its capacity to cope with problems in a messy polity.

NOTES

1. The tight centralization that is formally a part of the Israeli regime is loosened in practice, especially in so far as opportunities for local and even sub-local actors are concerned. See, for example, I. Sharkansky, 'Israel: A Metropolitan Nation-State', *Cities*, Vol. 14, No. 6 (1997), pp.363–70.
2. See, for example, G. Allison, *Essence of Decision: Explaining the Cuban Missile Crisis*, Boston: Little, Brown & Co., 1971; M. Crozier, *The Bureaucratic Phenomenon*, Chicago: University of Chicago Press, 1964; C. Debbasch, *Institutions administratives*, Paris: Librairie gnral de droit et de jurisprudence, 1966; A. Downs, *Inside Bureaucracy*, Boston: Little, Brown & Co, 1967; F. Heady, *Public Administration: A Comparative Perspective*, 3rd edn, Englewood Cliffs, NJ: Prentice-Hall, 1979; T. Lowi, *The End of Liberalism*, New York: Norton, 1969; T. Lowi, 'Public Policy and Bureaucracy in the United States and France', in D.E. Ashford, P. Katzenstein and T.J. Pempel (eds.), *Comparing Public Policies: New Concepts and Methods*, Beverly Hills: Sage Publications, pp.177–95.
3. See also, Y. Dror, 'Public Administration in Israel', in D.C. Rowat (ed.), *Public Administration in Developed Democracies: A Comparative Study*, New York: Marcel Dekker, 1988, pp.357–73.

4. Prime Minister's Office, *The Public–Professional Committee for the New Public Management, A Mandate,* Prime Minister's Office, 17 Feb. 2000. For an early attempt to initiate similar reforms, see I. Galnoor, D.H. Rosenbloom and A. Yaroni, 'Creating New Public Management Reforms: Lessons from Israel', *Administration and Society,* Vol. 30 (1998), pp.393–420.

5. C. Hood, 'A Public Management for All Seasons?', *Public Administration,* Vol. 69 (1991), pp.3–19; Z. Lan and D.H. Rosenbloom, 'Public Administration in Transition?', *Public Administration Review,* Vol. 52, No. 6 (1992), pp.535–8; J. Boston, J. Martin, P. June and W. Pat (eds.), *Public Management: The New Zealand Model,* Auckland: Oxford University Press, 1996.

6. For the impact NPM has had on recruitment and training of senior civil servants see M. Maor and H. Stevens, 'The Impact of New Public Management and European Integration on Recruitment and Training in the UK Civil Service, 1970–1995', *Public Administration,* Vol. 75, No. 3 (1997), pp.531–51; M. Maor, 'The Impact of European Integration and NPM on Recruitment and Training of Senior Public Officials: A Methodology', *Current Politics and Economics of Europe,* Vol. 7, No. 1 (1997), pp.59–81; M. Maor and G.W. Jones, 'Varieties of Administrative Convergence', *The International Journal of Public Sector Management,* Vol. 12, No. 1 (1998), pp.49–62; M. Maor, 'Recruitment and Training of Senior Civil Servants in Denmark and Norway, 1970–1995: The Impact of New Public Management and European Integration', *Current Politics and Economics of Europe,* Vol. 8, No. 4 (1999), pp.321–40; M. Maor, 'Recruitment and Training of Senior Civil Servants in Germany and the UK, 1970–1995: The Impact of New Public Management and European Integration', *Current Politics and Economics of Europe,* Vol. 8, No. 4 (1999), pp.341–55; M. Maor, 'A Comparative Perspective on Executive Development: Trends in 11 European Countries', *Public Administration,* Vol. 78, No. 1 (2000), pp.135–52.

7. For a similar experience abroad, see M. Maor, 'The Paradox of Managerialism', *Public Administration Review,* Vol. 59, No. 1 (1999), pp.5–18.

8. See, for example, B.S. Silberman, *Cages of Reason: The Rise of the Rational State in France, Japan, The United States and Great Britain,* Chicago: Chicago University Press, 1993.

The Development of the Israeli Government Offices

AHARON KFIR

INTRODUCTION

Israel's civil service, in general, and the structure of its government offices, in particular, have been fraught with problems ever since the state was established. In contrast to other spheres of public administration (for example, defence, agriculture, science, etc.) which are considered achievements and have acquired rational patterns, the idea is prevalent that the administrative structure of government offices and the civil service has not been blessed with either attainments or any great measure of rationality. Israel's first prime minister, David Ben-Gurion, once remarked, 'Let us be frank, administration is a trade we know not formerly, or at least, have not followed for centuries past. We have to practice a new craft, and almost create something out of nothing'.[1] Since independence there has been continuous criticism of the structure of government offices, and ongoing efforts and experiments aimed at introducing reforms and changes in this field.

The general impression is that the special and difficult conditions surrounding the establishment of the state (the War of Independence, the state of chaos wilfully created by the Mandate authorities, stress, the objective of absorbing a host of new immigrants, and the urgent need to create 'something out of nothing') precluded the instituting of a rational approach, political neutrality and advanced administration techniques in structuring office procedures.

Careful examination of the processes that brought about the current situation in government offices contradicts this opinion. It was not objective difficulties or the stresses of dramatic occurrences that were the cause of the defects and the operational difficulties of government offices. Despite the problems and considerable difficulties which the Jewish establishment was facing immediately prior to independence, a great deal of thought was given to the structure of the government service of the (future)

Aharon Kfir is Associate Professor of Public Administration and the Director of the Master of Science in Public Administration executive programme in the Department of Political Science at Haifa University.

independent state. The outcome of all this thought and planning was a well-founded structure for government offices imbued with formal Weberian characteristics, well able to stand the test of modern administrative methodology. The distortions in the structure of government offices and the shortcomings in performance stemmed, and continue for the most part, from non-compliance with the detailed original plans, rather than from any lack of plans or their not having been fully thought out.

Of the components influencing the efficiency of government administration, the organizational structure of government offices is pivotal, greatly determining the quality of administrative staff and orders, and fixing the degree by which policies and procedures are adapted to current technological data. Of course, even the best of organizational structures will not make up for a lack of all the other influencing factors. Improvements in the organizational structure must be carried out concomitant with the development and efficiency of skills in administrative personnel, raising the morale and degree of involvement of staff and the introduction of intelligent administrative approaches and procedures. For these the application of modern scientific policy methods and decision-making in government administration are needed. However, an appropriate organizational structure defining the number of offices, the divisions of functions between them, the determination of purposes, coordination and central control, could provide an important direct and immediate contribution to the quality of government administration. An efficient structure assists in overcoming obstacles (not only at the level of determining public policy, but also at the level of carrying it out) that arise from a multiplicity of offices, a duplication of duties and a lack of policy direction and control. An efficient structure can also serve as an incentive and aid in the introduction of improvements in other aspects of government administration, not only because of the reciprocal influence existing between the various components of the administrative structures, but also because it frees the upper echelons (as well as the middle echelons) from being occupied with comparisons and the constant efforts to overcome problems of coordination and combinations arising from a deficient structure. This failure to comply has been repeated with regard to those plans added subsequently in a haphazard manner. It may be assumed that certain trends that crystallized in the early years of the state have some bearing on the manner in which current problems are handled, in particular the modernization of administrative procedures. It is also to be assumed that administrative innovations are possible as long as they do not clash with basic established procedures.[2]

FORMATION OF THE GOVERNMENT OFFICE STRUCTURE

The structure and functioning of government offices in Israel were determined at the time of the establishment of the state on the basis of the traditions of the Jewish National Offices in the Yishuv (the Jewish community in Palestine), particularly the Jewish Agency and the Va'ad Leumi the Jewish National Council, the departments of the pre-state Mandatory authority, which also provided their infrastructure, with the exigencies of the political, social and economic problems that faced the new state also borne in mind. These characteristics and requirements were, by their nature, dynamic, and accordingly influence the later dynamism and functioning of the administration's structure.[3] The organized Jewish community in the Yishuv was composed of a number of formerly Ottoman organizations that functioned largely in cooperation and coordination with the Mandatory authority, and according to the level of the latter's involvement in their areas of activity.[4]

The procedure for appointment and allocation of functions was based on the 'key' system according to the proportional political strength of the different institutions. This system, though having the potential for independent government and providing arenas of economic and social advancement, was subject to much criticism.

The principal institutions of the Yishuv were the Jewish Agency and the Va'ad Leumi – the National Council, and together they represented the Jewish population before the Mandatory authority. The Jewish Agency was founded in 1929. Under the terms of the Mandate given by the League of Nations to the British Government in 1922, it was declared that, in order to implement the Balfour Declaration, a 'Jewish Agency' should be established. It was a partnership of Zionist and non-Zionist organizations. The Agency (together with the Va'ad Leumi) was to become the representative of the Jewish population in Palestine to the Mandatory authorities, and was the principal factor in creating the embryonic state. The Jewish Agency served as a kind of government within the government. Its departments were few in number, concentrated in their structure and practical in their activities, with a considerable disclarity of action between the elected and appointed personnel. The principal departments of the Agency were the Political Department (headed by Moshe Shertok-Sharett), the Economic Department (headed by Eliezer Kaplan), and the Settlement Department (headed by Levi Eshkol). Other departments dealt with the Treasury, labour, commerce and industry, manufacturing and light industry, *aliyah* (immigration) and youth, education and culture in the Diaspora, and information. (After the establishment of the state, the Agency continued to exist and several departments were added, such as public relations, Jerusalem development, and overseas radio broadcasts.)

The Delegates Congress (the Jewish community in Palestine's elected body, organized as 'Knesseth Israel')[5] had its policies carried out by the Va'ad Leumi. This body comprised 23 representatives, chosen annually at the Assembly of Representatives. Seven among them formed the

Executive Committee, which attended to current matters. The Va'ad was concerned with the provision and development of welfare, health and education services for the Jewish population. Its activities were carried out through its head offices in Jerusalem and local community committees in the various towns. The Va'ad Leumi also represented the 'Delegates Congress' to the Mandatory government, as well as performing such duties as given it by the Mandatory authority. The principal departments of the Va'ad Leumi were the political, community and rabbinate, health, education and culture and welfare, physical training, news media, and information. This organization was abolished at independence when most of its duties were transferred to the government, with some going to the Jewish Agency.

The Mandate administration operated on British colonial lines as laid down by London. The head of administration was the High Commissioner, appointed by the British Colonial Office and vested with wide legal authority. There were also government departments functioning bureaucratically with no public control whatsoever nor any orientation towards dependence. At the end of the Mandate the administrative organization was spread over 45 independent departments coordinated by a central secretariat. Compared with other colonial administrations, this establishment was relatively efficient, and it did a great deal for the development of the country, particularly at the local and district council level. At the termination of the Mandate only 4,800 of the 36,000 Mandate employees were Jewish, and these only in the lower positions (Statistical Yearbooks of the Jewish Agency).[6]

PLANNING OF THE GOVERNMENT ADMINISTRATION: STRUCTURE AND OPERATION

The structure of the administration and the allocation of responsibilities in the Jewish state was under consideration by the Yishuv leadership for many years, but particularly between 1943 and 1946. During this period a small committee headed by David Ben-Gurion was elected by the Agency and charged with preparing a plan to be presented to the 22nd Zionist Congress to take place in 1946. This proposal, which was comprised of general terms of reference for the structure and operation of the future Jewish state's government, was indeed submitted to the Congress.[7]

In the summer of 1947, when the imminence of the establishment of a Jewish state became more apparent, the awareness of the need to be properly organized grew. In September 1947, the Jewish Agency and the Va'ad Leumi decided to appoint a special body to deal with details of the structure and operation of the future state's government administration. Ben-Gurion, chairman of the Agency, headed this body, which was called Va'adat Matzav (Situation Committee). Together with Ben-Gurion were three other members of the Agency and four members of Va'ad Leumi. The committee was subsequently enlarged to a total of 13, equally representing the Jewish Agency and Va'ad Leumi.

The committee examined the operational procedures of the Mandate offices and planned the continuation of these operations within the framework of the future state's administration. It was understood from the outset that these 43 departments would be condensed into a smaller number of ministries. The committee appointed sub-committees with responsibility for specific departments. The sub-committees considered the aspects of the various problems in detail and delegated a specific member to each. The assistance of experts was provided to each member, thus bringing to each problem information and expertise on the functioning of these particular departments in other countries. The suggestions thus formulated were considered by the sub-committee, which crystallized them in each case into a single portfolio that dealt with such details as personnel, budget and equipment required. The Va'adat Matzav met only infrequently, a factor that acted against smooth operation. There were three stages of preparatory work: (1) the period prior to the United Nations decision; (2) the period between the UN decision and March 1948; and (3) from March 1948 until the declaration of the state.

The transition from one stage to the next was neither unilateral nor clearly defined. By the same token the transition to a further stage did not absolve the committee from its occupation with the problems of the previous one, in the main those connected with the essential objective – planning of the government administration of the future state.

An example of a preliminary plan to obviate chaotic conditions in the operation of departments and government units is to be found in a memorandum dated 23 January 1948, prepared by Dr Yehoshua Greenbaum of the legal department of the Va'adat Matzav. The memorandum which details the departments, their functions and how these are to be carried out and supervised, stated *inter alia*:

> There is a need for detailed planning in order to take over the various departments of the Palestine Government. This should be done whether or not the Government will be prepared to transfer the administration to us or to the executive committee. This plan must lay down which offices will take over each department, either with cooperation of the current officials, without it or even against their will. This operation must be carried out in cooperation with the Haganah (the Jewish Defence Organization) in order to obviate sabotage by either Arabs or British. The operation must be carried out with precision and speed in a 'commando' like manner in order to eliminate possible chaos.[8]

Preliminary Proposals

Preliminary proposals for the structure of government offices and local authorities were crystallized by the sub-committees in January 1948, and were based on the recommendations of the experts only, without any interference from the politicians. The planners were thus comparatively free, without any outside sectarian or party influences, and could focus on administrative logic and the rules of administration in forming their proposals.

Under the terms of the proposals (submitted to the Va'adat Matzav on 21 January 1948), the government would be comprised of a prime minister, 12 ministers and 12 deputy ministers. These 25 posts would be political appointments (the deputy ministers would participate in cabinet meetings only in the event of matters concerning their particular portfolio arising when the responsible minister, because of illness or being out of the country, could not attend).

The proposed allocation of portfolios was as follows: Prime Minister's Office (including an independent Statistical Office); Treasury; Foreign Affairs (including a department of information in conjunction with the Zionist Organization); Commerce, Industry and Agriculture; Interior (including police, prisons and local authorities); Education and Culture (including broadcasting); Labour; Health and Social Work; Public Works, Transport and Town Planners; Justice; Development and Planning (to deal with development plans, relinquishing of current positions in cooperation with the Zionist Organization); and Defence.

Noteworthy are the proposals to establish a special Ministry of Development and Planning unhampered by the stress of current problems, able to concentrate on long-range planning, and having control over all inter-ministerial functioning; and to cooperate with the World Zionist Organization in matters of immigration and absorption. The former proposal was not subsequently repeated.

In addition, the establishment of three inter-ministerial committees was proposed: (1) Immigration and Absorption   to function within the framework of the World Zionist Organization and the government of the Jewish state, to be headed by the prime minister; (2) Economic Affairs – to coordinate economic functions, including the Ministries of Economic Affairs, Foreign Affairs, and Trade and Industry; to be headed by the minister of economics; and (3) Human Resources Committee to coordinate manpower recruitment and development.

There were other opinions expressed at the committee, but finally a compromise was accepted. This compromise was typical of the approach of the politicians on the Va'adat Matzav, who avoided as much as possible taking decisions in principle even if such decisions were necessary to ensure a rational future function and structure. They preferred to avoid conflict and to protect their sectarian interests.

The sub-committee continued to consider in detail the various proposals made by the experts, based on research of the current situation, assessment of future requirements, and comparison with the situation in other countries. These discussions went on despite many difficulties, such as problems of communication and travel between Jerusalem and Tel Aviv, and the differences of opinion between members of the Jewish Agency and members of the Va'ad Leumi as to their respective entitlements. The difficulties continued until April, and were resolved at the meeting of the Executive Committee with the election of the Committee of 13. The committee accomplished its tasks and presented a detailed proposal for the structure, civil service and budget for the Jewish state. The proposal of the committee, prepared by their advisers (largely because of the difficulties in convening the Va'adat Matzav in the final stages of preparation) was to a great extent based on rational administrative procedural considerations. This is attested by Ze'ev Sharf, convenor of the committee of experts, who stated: 'This proposal was prepared solely by officials and we were therefore relieved when preparing the proposal, of any influence by the party representatives. Accordingly we based the proposal on the accepted rules for public service unhampered by personal or party considerations.'[9]

The Legal Council was the largest sub-committee. Chaired by B. Joseph and M. Eliash, it recommended that Jewish philosophy become the basis of the civil legal system. It further recommended that new statutes be enacted in regard to the civil service. The council was unanimous in its recommendation to eliminate the religious courts. A proposal by Dr A. Freeman that two secular judges sit together with the presiding rabbi was rejected, and the proposer joined the majority decision. With both Ben-Gurion and Shertock (Sharett) defending the autonomy of the Muslims, Rabbi Fishman (Mimone) demanded that rabbinic courts be allowed to continue. It was finally agreed to let matters stand as they were. Ben-Gurion proposed this as a compromise following the proposal by Dr Warhaftig that Halacha (Jewish Law) extends to areas of the civil legal system and should replace British law.

The Legal Council faced strong opposition from the Histadrut the Federation of Trade Unions. Its proposal to inaugurate a comprehensive population register as an adjunct to the Ministry of Justice, to replace the many different registers kept by a variety of offices, was opposed on the grounds that it would cause the retrenchment of many officials. The committee suggested that the Histadrut have no say in labour relations. They underestimated the power of the Histadrut, which was against the formulation of regulations to govern the discipline and responsibility of government employees. None of these proposals was carried. Ideas of efficiency, rationality and wide-ranging impartiality of government service were shattered by the impact of a 'Jewish War'.[10]

The Legal Council recommended an emphasis on principal laws and that there be a minimum of administrative regulations a basic democratic principle. The Knesseth proved itself to be an ineffective legislative body, lacking in consensus and self-confidence and given to delays and foot-dragging. It in fact developed in the opposite direction: promulgating a great many by-laws.

The Government Personnel Sub-Committee only commenced its work in February 1948, but was one of the first to submit its findings to the plenum as early as the beginning of March. In the main, the sub-committee concerned itself with the question of the appointment of officials in the Jewish state and the safeguarding of the employees of the National Organizations and the Mandate. The attitude towards Jewish employees of the Mandate was ambivalent: on the one hand their expertise, knowledge and ability were valuable, on the other hand they were looked on askance because of their loyalty to the Mandate. (Preference for employees of the National Organizations stemmed for the most part from loyalty and affiliation, principally political.) The sub-committee then proposed that Mandate officials employed in departments transferred to the future state would continue in government service after their loyalty and personal behaviour had been examined. Every previous employee of the Mandate or National Organizations retained would continue to work under the same conditions and with same remuneration already received.[11]

Government Structure – Proposal by the Va'adat Matzav – April 1948

In mid-April 1948 the Va'adat Matzav, together with the executives of the Va'ad Leumi and the Jewish Agency, submitted a detailed proposal for the structure, personnel and budgets of the various government departments, entitled *The Government Administration of the Hebrew State*. It was submitted to the committee (Va'adat Matzav) for consideration and approval in the hope that it would become the basis for government structure which was to come into being the following month. It stated that, 'Whilst not entirely complete, they ['the sub-committees' proposals] do embody an attempt of many people to create an administration for the State which will be able to effectively fulfil the duties and obligations of a modern government administration'.[12] The proposal was for a government of 13 ministries, each with several detailed departments. The ministries were: Prime Minister; Finance and Economy; Interior; Foreign Affairs; Trade and Industry; Agriculture; Labour; Communications and Transport; Public Works and Technical Services; Education and Culture; Social Services; Justice; Defence. In addition it was suggested that four independent bodies be established: (1) a Government Controller – to be responsible directly to the house of elected representatives; (2) a Department of Statistics – to be responsible to the Prime Minister's Office;

(3) a Government Printers – administrative attachment not yet determined; (4) an independent Civil Service Commission.

The Va'adat Matzav encountered difficulty in dealing with the proposal of the secretariat (because of communication and transport problems as well as internal disagreements between representatives of the Jewish Agency and those of the Va'ad Leumi). Only one of the decisions of the Zionist Executives taken on 12 April 1948 regarding the establishment of the Council of 37 (National Council) and the Committee of 13 (National Executives) was at all considered in the proposal made by the secretariat of the Va'adat Matzav.

Ben-Gurion, who had been appointed by the Zionist Executives to head the Committee of 13, convened the first meeting of that committee for 18 April 1948. The invitation read:

> In the name of the Executive of the Jewish Agency I have the honor to invite you to the first meeting of the Committee of 13, to whom the authorities of the organizations, with the sanction of the Executives of the Zionist Organizations, have delegated the conducting of all the affairs of the Yishuv and the establishment of the Jewish state until such time as there be elections to the body of the state. The Committee of 13 is responsible to the Council of 37.

The following day Ben-Gurion wrote to Sharf stating that the leadership wanted to be assured that all the necessary arrangements would be made and that there be a person to whom all queries could be addressed, and accordingly he was appointing Sharf to be interim secretary for National Administration. The National Administration at its meeting of 21 April was briefed by Sharf on the proposals for the structure of the government. At a second meeting on 12 May the proposal for the 13 ministerial posts was approved.

THE INTERIM GOVERNMENT

The declaration of the state and the establishment of the interim government were preceded by several further discussions. Under the terms of the decision taken by the National Executive and the National Council at their final meeting on 12 May, the interim government came to power on Sunday 16 May 1948. A declaration drafted at this meeting, which ultimately became Government Order No. 1 of 1948, stated that, with the dissolution of the British Mandate in the land of Israel, the National Executive would function as the interim government of the state of Israel and would continue to function as such until such time as there be an elected government for the Jewish state.[13]

The interim government's organizational structure and allocation of portfolios differed from that recommended by the Va'adat Matzav and that which had been determined a mere few days earlier. There were now 17 portfolios: Prime Minister (David Ben-Gurion); Defence (David Ben-Gurion); Treasury and Economy (Eliezer Kaplan); Foreign Affairs (Moshe Sharrett (Shartok)); Interior (Itzchak Greenbaum); Justice (Pinchas Rozen (Rozenblatt)); Agriculture (Aharon Zisling); Commerce, Industry and Supply (Peretz Bernstein); Labour and Construction (Mordechai Ben-Tov); Welfare (Itche Meir Levin); Transport and Communication (David Remez); Health (Moshe Shapira); Immigration (Moshe Shapira); Police (Bechor Shitreet); Minorities (Bechor Shitreet); Religions (Yehuda Leib Fishman (Maimon)); and War Casualties (Yehuda Leib Fishman (Maimon)).

The main changes were a division of the social services into two portfolios (namely, Health and Welfare); an aggregation of public works and technical services into a Labour portfolio; an elimination of the portfolios for Education and Culture; and a creation of five new portfolios (Religious Affairs, War Casualties, Police, Minorities and Immigration).

While it was obvious that there were bound to be changes in the proposed allocation of portfolios, it is noteworthy to record how easily the major deviations from the original proposal were made. Among them the allocation of responsibility for functions such as education, health and welfare to non-government bodies and the inclusion of a Ministry of Police was unparalleled then in any democratic country. Also unclear was the combination of labour, which has a social function, with public works, which is distinctly technical.

These changes, most of which had a deleterious effect on the structure, efficiency and functioning of the ministries the ill effects of which are still being felt in certain ministries to this day did not stem from any positive consideration nor from the need to find more ministerial posts (there were still only 13 ministers). The main causes were that the prime minister did not give a great deal of value to government administration, it being a civilian arena as opposed to the military and security frameworks, and that political and personal demands were complied with in order to maintain an atmosphere of tranquillity in the coalition.[14]

Thus, the pressing need to concentrate all social services within one framework was not satisfied as the minister designated to social services, because of his own state of health, did not want to have the responsibility for the health portfolio. The recommendation that public works and technical services be a separate portfolio was defeated by the minister of labour's wish for wider authority; the minister appointed to the Interior Ministry, which included the Department of Police, refused to take on the latter unless it also controlled internal security, which was Ben-Gurion's responsibility, at the time. A separate Ministry of Police was created, owing to Ben-Gurion's firm opposition to surrendering authority over internal security. The Ministry of Religious Affairs was established as a gesture by Ben-Gurion to Rabbi Fishman (Maimon) who had insisted on the Jewish state having a Ministry of Jewish Religion. The other ministries were established in order to maintain a balanced division in the coalition, which would otherwise have disturbed the above-mentioned changes.[15]

The establishment of additional ministries by the interim and subsequent governments stemmed from political considerations, not objective needs or rational administrative requirements. As a rule the solution of personal or party political problems was the awarding of a ministerial position to minor political parties.

From the political–legal perspective, introducing a change in the structure of governmental ministries is easy enough, consequently encouraging its use as a means to solve various problems. The assignment of ministerial positions and governmental portfolios to members of the government is done at the time of formation, and the Knesset discusses the programme and approves the positions' assignment. Yet, acting in accordance with the law the government has the authority to merge separate ministries, divide them, eliminate them or establish new ones. The government may also change the assignment of positions to the various ministers, or reassign a certain duty or prerogative. There is no need to pass a law in order to form a new governmental office or to abolish it, and until the 1958 Government Formation Law was passed, a mere notification of any of these changes to the Knesset was sufficient. The new law demands that the government will also obtain the Knesset's approval. The Government Formation Law does not deal with the number of ministers and with their governmental positions at all (except for two positions – the prime minister and the minister of justice). Chapter 8(e) of the Budget Law describes the procedure for transfer of funds in case any change occurs in the structure of the offices or in the ministers' positions. The changes in and deviations from the institutional committee's recommendations consisted not only of changes in the number of ministries, but also in the number of public officials and sub-units.

The Va'adat Matzav had recommended that the number of departments and officials be kept low until the establishment of a central authority that would determine, in a sound and rational manner, the functions and selection of officials. However, there was no civil service commission to act as a brake at the time when the government officials were being appointed and each minister did as he wished.

The interim government functioned until after the elections (February 1949). At its seventh meeting, Ben-Gurion submitted the list of the first coalition government (comprising the following parties: Mapai, Religious Front, Progressive and the Sepharadim). There were 12 ministers holding 17 portfolios: Prime Minister (David Ben-Gurion); Defence (David Ben-Gurion); Foreign Affairs (Moshe Shertok (Sharett)); Treasury and Economy (Eliezer Kaplan); Commerce, Industry and Supply (Peretz

Bernstein); Education and Culture (Zalman Shazar); Labour and National Insurance (Golda Meir); Transport (David Remez); Rationing, Supply and Agriculture (Dov Joseph); Interior (Moshe Shapiro); Health (Moshe Shapiro); Immigration (Moshe Shapiro); Religion (Leib Fishman (Maimon)); War Casualties (Leib Fishman (Maimon)); Welfare (Itzchak Meir Levin); Justice (Pinchas Rozen (Rozenblatt)), and Police (Behor Shitreet).

TABLE 1
ISRAEL GOVERNMENTS 1948–96

The Government and Dates of Foundation	No. of Offices	No. of Ministers	Comments
The Temporary 16.5.48–10.3.49	17	13	Did not include the Education and Culture Ministry.
1st Government 10.3.49–30.10.50	17	12	The Ministry of Minority was closed. Supply and Rationing Ministry was added.
2nd Government 30.10.50–8.10.51	17	13	The Ministry of Supply and Rationing became the Ministry of Commerce and Industry.
3rd Government 8.10.51–24.12.52	16	13	These ministries were closed: Immigration, War Casualties; the Ministry of Mail was added.
4th Government 23.12.52–26.1.54	16	16	
5th Government 26.1.54–29.6.55	17	16	The Ministry of Development was added.
6th Government 29.6.55–3.11.55	17	12	
7th Government 3.11.55–7.1.58	17	16	
8th Government 7.1.58–17.12.59	17	16	
9th Government 17.12.59–2.11.61	17	16	
10th Government 2.11.61–26.6.63	18	16	The Ministry of Housing was added.
11th Government 26.6.63–22.12.64	18	17	The position of vice-prime minister was added – Abba Eban.

12th Government 22.12.64–12.1.66	19	17	The Ministry of Tourism was added.
13th Government 12.1.66–17.3.69	19	19	
14th Government 17.3.69–15.12.69	20	22	The Ministry of Absorption was added.
15th Government 15.12.69–10.3.74	20	22	
16th Government 10.3.74–3.6.74	20	25	
17th Government 3.6.74–20.6.77	20	22	The Ministry of Development was closed and the Ministry of Information was added.
18th Government 20.6.77–5.8.81	20	19	The following ministries were closed: Police, Information, Tourism, Energy and Infrastructure.
19th Government 5.8.81–10.10.83	17	19	The ministries of Labour and Welfare merged into one office – the Ministry of Welfare.
20th Government 10.10.83–13.9.84	20	20	The Ministry of Economics and Coordination, the Ministry of Tourism and the Ministry of Science and Development were added.
21st Government 13.9.84–20.10.86	20	20	
22nd Government 20.10.86–22.12.88	21	25	The Ministry of Police was added.
23rd Government 22.12.88–11.6.90	21	24	
24th Government 11.6.90–13.7.92	23	26	The Ministry of Quality of Environment was added and the Ministry of Science and Development was changed to the Ministry of Science and Technology. The Ministry of Jerusalem Affairs was added.
25th Government 13.7.92–22.11.95	22	20	The Ministry of Jerusalem Affairs was closed.
26th Government 22.11.95–18.6.96	21	20	The Ministry of Economics was closed. The Ministry of Police was changed to the Ministry of Internal Security.
27th Government 18.6.96–17.2.01	21	18	The Ministry of Energy and Infrastructure was changed to the Nationality Infrastructure.
28th Government 17.2.01–	22	24	The Ministry of Jerusalem Affairs was added.

In the course of time there were many changes in the structure of the government ministries. Some were eliminated (Minorities and War Casualties, the ministries of Immigration, Supply and Rationing, Development and Information) and others were created (Posts, Housing, Tourism, Absorption, Energy, Infrastructure, Economy and Science and Development). There were many transfers of functions and departments from one ministry to another, but the basic flaws: combining welfare with technical services into a single framework, or the maintaining of separate offices with overlapping functions, were not eradicated for many years. Table 1 shows the changes in the Israeli government's structure in the years 1948–96.

THE CHARACTERISTICS OF THE GOVERNMENT OFFICES' STRUCTURE IN ISRAEL

The essential characteristics of the structure of the government offices are thus: a profusion of government offices; a dispersal of similar duties among various offices; a lack of preplanning and direction; and a lack of coordination and centralized supervision. Each of these aspects works against the establishment of proper processes of execution. The profusion of government offices, for example, has particularly negative effects. It creates difficulty in determining and implementing policy when such falls within the purview of different ministries. Diversification necessitates the creation of coordinating organizations whose functioning, since they have no power of enforcement, depends on the goodwill of the participants. The government, rather than exercising its authority in differences of opinion between ministries, has preferred to act as a coordinating body between opposing opinions and different approaches.[16] It also leads to insufficient provision of services. The citizen, in trying to solve a problem, is often required to contact several bodies. He or she is often sent from office to office and suffers as a result of inter-office rivalries. A derived consequence is that some take advantage of this overlapping.[17] Furthermore, the existence of redundant offices has resulted in the wasting of vital resources – manpower, services and equipment.

The profusion of government offices is problematic also in terms of the collation of offices and distribution of duties. In the collation of functions and the allocation of duties between government offices, mistakes were already made at the time when the state was established. Organizational frameworks such as manpower and procedures were taken over from existing organizations (the National Institution, the Mandate bureaucracy and others), each different in structure. These frameworks continue to operate separately but in a parallel track without sufficient coordination and adjustment. This has led to increased duplication and lack of clarity.[18]

Finally, the profusion of government offices leads to problems of coordination and supervision. In every complex organization there is a need for central coordination and supervision. All the more so in so complex and diversified an organization as the government establishment. From the time of the establishment of the state, the government offices have suffered from the paucity of directive organization, coordination and supervision. Despite the coalition structure of the government, which made centralized supervision and direction difficult, there was room for the establishment of staff units (to function in an advisory capacity to the formal office bearers) at a suitable level under the aegis of the prime minister. These units have been able to strengthen inter-office coordination, improve the quality of policy-making and ensure a great deal of supervision. At present, however, there are some government offices which function unilaterally with complete independence, outside any framework of cooperation and coordination.[19]

CONCLUSION

It may be assumed that the relative strength of the sectional powers, the absence of any critical evaluation in the matter of government administration, and the lack of a central influencing factor, all mitigated both the acceptance of the recommendations of the Va'adat Matzav and the creation of a rational, efficient structure of government administration, and created the opportunity for inefficient practices to become inherent.

Since the establishment of the state and the creation of the structure of its government administration there have been numerous proposals for change. Almost every one of these proposals was aimed at the elimination of three main shortcomings: curtailment of the number of government offices; reorganization of the functions of the various offices in order to maximize coordination; development of directional planning and coordinate supervision of activities – all of which the Va'adat Matzav had tried to obviate in its 1948 proposals.

NOTES

1. David Nachmias and David H. Rosenbloom, *Bureaucratic Culture: Citizens and Administrators in Israel*, New York: St Martins Press, 1989, p.47.
2. Amos Perlmutter, 'Anatomy of Political Institutionalization, the Case of Israel and Some Comparative Analysis', *Occasional Papers in International Affairs*, No. 25 (Feb. 1970), p.26 (Harvard University).
3. S.N. Eisenstadt, 'Institutionalization and Change', *American Sociological Review*, Vol. 29 (1964), pp.235–48.
4. Governmental administration was influenced, to a certain degree, by other sources including Turkish. Partly this influence can be recognized today in the legal system and courts structure and performance in local government administration.

5. The British Mandate administration gave in 1928 full authority to the Jewish-organized population in Palestine ('Knesseth Israel') to manage affairs of religion, education, welfare, health and social assistance.
6. On characteristics of the British Mandate administration, see Arian David, *The First Five Years of the Israeli Civil Service*, Jerusalem: Civil Service Commission, 1955.
7. *The Zionist Organization and Jewish Agency for Palestine*, Reports of the Executive submitted to the 22nd Zionist Congress at Basel, Jerusalem: Archive of the Zionist Organization, Dec. 1946.
8. Ze'ev Sharf, *Three Days, An Account of the Last Days of the British Mandate and the Birth of Israel*, London: W.H. Allen, 1962 (trans. from 1951 Hebrew edn), pp.49–53.
9. See *The Administration of the Hebrew State – A Proposal of the Structure, Staff and Budget*, Jerusalem: Jewish Agency, April 1948 (in Hebrew).
10. On the work of the Legal Sub-Committee, see Files Nos. 215–17 of Va'adat Matzav, National Archives, Jerusalem.
11. On the design and development of the civil service, see, Jacob Reuveny, *The Israeli Public Administration – Civil Service in Israel in the Years 1948–1973*, Tel Aviv: Massada Pub., 1974 (in Hebrew).
12. Ibid.
13. See File No. 455, National Archives, Jerusalem.
14. These evaluations are based on a few interviews with some of the active members of the sub-committees, including Ze'ev Sharf, Haim Cohen, Hana Even-Tov, David Arian.
15. Ze'ev Sharf in his book *Three Days* (note 8 above) writes (p.50 of the Hebrew edition) that Mr Greenbaum – appointed minister of interior – refused to include the police within his office, because he was always persecuted by the police as a revolutionary in Russia, in Poland and in Palestine, and does not wish to be connected with them in the free state of Israel. But, in an interview with me in 1972 he said clearly that Greenbaum wanted very much to be in charge of the police but on one condition, that it should include the interior security, which Ben-Gurion refused. This was the real reason for his refusal.
16. Yechezkel Dror, 'The Government of National Unity', OT, No. 6, 1968 (in Hebrew).
17. See Aharon Kfir, *Administrative Procedures of Export*, Haifa: University of Haifa, Yozma, 1987 (in Hebrew).
18. On the splitting of the treatment with new immigrants among 13 governmental offices and agencies, see Aharon Kfir, *Organization and Management – Design and Change*, Tel Aviv: Tcherikover, 1997, pp.329–52 (in Hebrew).
19. On central guidance and control on the Israeli government offices, see ibid., pp.353–72; Aharon Kfir, *Managing of Organizations – Theory and Practice*, Tel Aviv: Tcherikover, 1998, pp.155–82 (in Hebrew). *Report of the Committee for Review of the Civil Service and Government Funded Bodies* ('Kubersky Report'), Jerusalem: Government Printer, 1980, pp.59–63, 124–37 (in Hebrew).

Administrative Power in Israel

EVA ETZIONI-HALEVY

ADMINISTRATIVE POWER AS ELITE POWER

Focusing on the power of the state administration, this chapter's thesis is that in Israel this power is considerable, but not autonomous. Rather, there is a close connection between the administrative elite and the political elite, whereby the former is dependent on the latter. By virtue of this close but unequal connection, administrative power is linked to party politics, and works in its service. This creates severe problems for Israeli democracy.

Despite recent attempts at administrative reforms, this system has persisted since the establishment of the state (and even before), up until the present. Over the years there have been various changes and developments. But there has been no fundamental transformation of the arrangements, whereby – in some major parts of the state bureaucracy – administrative power serves as a handmaiden to politics, to the detriment of the quality of democracy.

This thesis is elaborated in the framework of a democratic-elite theoretical perspective, presented in the wake of the theories of Max Weber, Gaetano Mosca, Joseph Schumpeter and Raymond Aron, and by this author.[1]

Following Weber's analysis, this perspective emphasizes that the state administration, or bureaucracy, is one of the most formidable organizations in modern society, which wields considerable power. This power, however, is not dispersed evenly throughout the administration, but is concentrated mainly at the top, in the hands of the administrative elite.

An elite is defined as a relatively small group of people that wields inordinate power and influence on the basis of its control of resources. In contemporary society, we may distinguish between several types of elites, including the political elite (the government, as well as the members of parliament and various other high-ranking politicians within political parties) and the administrative elite (the holders of the top positions in the state administration).[2]

Eva Etzioni-Halevy is Professor of Political Sociology at the Department of Sociology and Anthropology, Bar-Ilan University. She is also a fellow of the Academy of the Social Sciences in Australia. Her speciality is democratic theory and the role of elites and bureaucracy in democracy and democratization.

The administrative elite wields power on the basis of at least three types of resources. It does so, first, on the basis of the organizational resources of the state administration. This body (to various degrees) organizes or oversees various aspects of citizens' lives, such as education, health services, quality control of consumer products, immigration and much more. Those in charge of this organization thus also hold sway over citizens' lives.

The power concentrated at the top of the state bureaucracy is based, second, on material resources. These have their source mainly in taxes and levies, as well as in profits of government-owned companies. The state administration is responsible for both the collection of these monies, and their reallocation for a variety of purposes. The guidelines for this collection and allocation are set by the government. But the actual tasks of gathering and handing out the funds are carried out by the bureaucracy, and the discretion which its heads may use in this respect serves as an additional source of power for them.

No less important are the symbolic resources which the state bureaucracy has at its disposal. These include systems of information on individual citizens, as well as on the workings of the state and its administration itself, all of which have been greatly enhanced by recent computerization. These types of information, too, may be used at the discretion of bureaucrats, and this greatly enhances their power.

THE POWER OF THE ADMINISTRATIVE ELITE IN ISRAEL

The power of systems of information as described above is true for the administrative elites in all contemporary – including Western – states, but it is especially true for Israel. For, in this country, the bureaucracy is especially intrusive, compared to its counterparts in many Western democracies. Despite a trend of liberalization, here the state administration still controls economic activity to a greater extent than is the case in most Western countries. Notwithstanding a trend of decentralization, the Ministry of Education still guides educational policy, more than is the case in countries such as the United States and Britain.[3]

Also, in Israel, the material resources that the state bureaucracy controls are relatively larger than is customary in the West. This is so, because in Israel such resources are derived not only from taxes, levies and profits – as in other countries – but also from (albeit shrinking) contributions from Jews abroad, and from massive American foreign aid. Hence, the funds that are allocated at the discretion of top-level administrators are of an unusually large magnitude.

Finally, and partly for security reasons, Israel's state agencies gather more information about citizens than is considered tolerable in most democracies. While this information is not generally misused, it is still a potential source of power in the hands of those who have charge of it. What is important, however, is not only how much power the administrative elite has at its disposal, but also, in whose service it is used.

ADMINISTRATIVE POWER – A DEMOCRATIC DILEMMA

In this respect, administrative power generates a democratic dilemma. As democratic elite theory emphasizes, a powerful administrative elite, that is autonomous from the elected government, poses a threat to the quality of democracy. But an administrative elite that is connected to the government and uses its power at the behest of its members forms an even greater threat to the quality of democracy.

As conceived here, democracy includes, at the very least, free competitive elections by universal suffrage and basic civil liberties. These are the basic criteria that distinguish a democratic from a non-democratic regime. Beyond this, however, there are qualitative differences between democracies. According to some observers such as Buckhart and Lewis-Beck,[4] this quality may be assessed by the degree to which elections are meaningful, as well as fair.

Elections are meaningful when those elected hold the power to govern not only formally, but also in actual practice. That is to say, when the real power is in fact vested in those who are elected, rather than in others, who are not. And elections are fair when they are based on fair electoral campaigns. That is, they cannot be manipulated, for instance, by government politicians handing out state resources and benefits to individuals, in return for political/electoral support.

In the democratic state as it has actually taken shape, however, only the government, as holder of political power, is elected. By contrast, those who hold administrative power govern without being elected. A high quality of democracy thus requires that the power of non-elected administrators be under the control of the elected government. Only in this manner may the government use its power to carry out the policies, for the implementation of which it has been elected. Any administrative power that is exempt from government control thus detracts from the quality of democracy.

A high quality of democracy also requires, however, that elections be fair, and not subject to manipulation by the government. Yet, this is precisely what happens when the state administration is subordinated to the government. For in this case, government politicians may use it as an instrument of manipulation. They may utilize it in handing out benefits, so as to marshal support for themselves at the next election.

The subjection of administrative power to government politicians is frequently achieved through political appointments and promotions in the civil service. For mandarins, who owe their appointments and promotions to the government's political leaders, are under an obligation to them. In addition, once appointed, they are still dependent on these politicians for maintaining their positions, and also for their subsequent promotions. Hence they may be relied upon to serve their patrons' interests, by conniving in their political manipulations for electoral purposes. Politically dominated administrative power thus makes inroads into the fairness of elections, and thereby detracts from the quality of democracy.

TWO TYPES OF ADMINISTRATIVE POWER

This argument may be clarified by means of a distinction between two types of administrative power. The first type prevails in an administration in which appointments and promotions are made by persons (usually civil servants) who are themselves independent from government politicians. Even here, there is no total separation between administration and politics, since any administrative action has political implications. But in this system, administrators have no particular motivation or obligation to serve the interests of politicians. The second type of administrative power prevails in a system in which the administrative elite is linked to the political elite of the government, by being appointed by it, or under its sponsorship. Hence it is likely to exert its power in those politicians' interests.

A few centuries ago, when state administrations in the West were in their first stages of development, they were all of the second type. Political and administrative powers were not clearly distinguished from each other, appointments and promotions were partisan, and administrative power was employed in the service of politics. In the course of time, Western bureaucracies developed in different directions. Some, such as those of Belgium and Italy, grew in size, but largely retained their political mould. Others, such as those of Britain and Australia, introduced a much clearer separation between administrative and political power.

In addition, some intermediate types developed. In the United States, for instance, the major part of the bureaucracy underwent a process of depoliticization. But its top layer (comprising some 4,000–5,000 officials) has remained overtly party political. It is formally attached to the political elite that is in power at any given time, coming in and leaving the administration together with it.

A comparative study conducted by the author demonstrates that in countries in which administrative power remained subservient to politics, various electoral manipulations and malpractices flourished, and were perpetuated for many years.[5] And only in those countries in which administrative power gained at least some autonomy from politics have such electoral malpractices atrophied.

THE CONNECTION BETWEEN ADMINISTRATIVE AND POLITICAL POWER IN ISRAEL

Israel belongs to the type of country in which administrative power has remained closely connected with, and subservient to, politics. Because of the large-scale resources of which the Israeli state administration has control, it has (as previously noted) accumulated formidable power *vis-à-vis* its citizens. But the bureaucracy's control of such large resources has also increased the motivation of government politicians to subjugate it to their own ends. Hence the administrative elite's power, *vis-à-vis* the citizens, is a source of its weakness, *vis-à-vis* politicians.

The subjugation of the administration to government political power has been ensured through political appointments and promotions in particular – but not only – to top and key positions in the administration. And it has found expression in the consequent allocation of benefits for political purposes. Mostly, no outright electoral bribery is involved (although this, too, has happened occasionally). Rather, the system is one of 'cast thy bread upon the waters, for in the next election though shalt find it'.

Unlike in the United States, where political appointments at the top of the civil service are the official practice, in Israel, appointments and promotions, even at the top of the bureaucracy, are (with a very few exceptions), formally non-partisan, and dependent solely on merit. Hence they are to be effected following advertisement of the positions. In fact, however, this formally meritocratic procedure is frequently circumvented. And, unlike in the United States, where political appointees in the bureaucracy leave their positions when their political sponsors are voted out of office, in Israel, bureaucrats hold tenure, and cannot be dismissed. But when their political patrons lose an election, they are frequently displaced from their previous key positions, and pushed out into the margins. Thereby, while they retain their salaries, they are deprived of much of their power. And this adds to their motivation to do their utmost, so that the political elite of the government party which sponsored them be re-elected.

Consequently, while multi-party elections are a well-established procedure, the fairness of elections has been impaired by improper (and occasionally corrupt) allocations of money or its equivalent, with the collaboration of the administration.

THE ROOTS OF THE SYSTEM

The roots of the system are to be found in the pre-state, Yishuv, era. Specifically, it has its origin in the authority of self-government, also known as the 'National Institutions', set up by the budding Jewish community, under British Mandatory rule. This authority's bureaucracy had no system of entry based on objective qualifications, and appointments in it were overtly party political. The largest party was the Labour Party – Mapai – which held hegemony in the National Institutions, and also had the largest chunk of administrative positions at its disposal. However, Mapai was not the only beneficiary of the system. Appointments were made by the party-key, which means that all parties that cooperated with the authority were allocated positions according to their electoral size.

As a consequence, the National Institutions' bureaucracy was involved in the allocation of large-scale funds (most of which came from contributions of Jews in the Diaspora) to parties and party-connected political bodies. This created the 'pillarization' of political parties: to gain political support, they did not rely on ideological persuasion alone. Rather, they sought to bind supporters to themselves by impressive networks of banks, housing construction companies, loan societies, economic concerns, employment and health services and the like. Thus, they became supporting pillars of people's entire lives. And the people who relied on such parties throughout their life cycles also tended to bestow on them their allegiance and their votes.

Since Mapai was the largest party, which held sway over the largest part of the administration in the National Institutions, it was able to secure the biggest funds for itself and the bodies connected with it, including the Labour Federation – the Histadrut. But other parties benefited as well. These included not only other labour parties, but also the religious parties, and the right-wing citizens' parties. And only one party, the Revisionist Party, did not participate in this procedure of partisan appointments and allocations.

THE BEGINNING OF THE STATE ERA

With the establishment of the state in 1948, the newly created state administration largely perpetuated the patterns it had inherited from its predecessor, the 'National Institutions'. In 1959 a new law was enacted, and subsequently new civil service regulations came into effect, which were designed to mould the new bureaucracy according to the British blueprint. Henceforward, positions were to be advertised, and candidates were to be selected solely by merit. Nonetheless, senior appointments, and a large part of the more junior ones, remained party political.

In the 1960s, almost a third of the senior appointments were made without prior advertising of the positions. Also, advertisements for vacancies were frequently 'sewn up',[6] so as to fit the qualifications of candidates, who had been preselected on the basis of their political affiliations.

Hence, senior administrators continued to serve their political patrons by channelling benefits to the public through political parties and party-related bodies, such as the Histadrut. This made it possible for the pillarization of parties to continue, and for patronage to serve as an enticement for political backing.

The first years of statehood saw a mass immigration in which the country's population was tripled within a few years. The masses of new immigrants were absorbed by a variety of Histadrut and party-linked institutions: housing corporations, labour exchanges, banks and the like. This enabled the parties to try and tie the new immigrants to themselves, through a network of employment services and other job placements, as well as economic aid, especially for (the extortionately expensive) housing.

The horn of plenty was, once again, chiefly in the hands of Mapai, and to a lesser extent in the hands of its allied labour parties. Since it was the chief party in power, it had under its control a major part of the state administration, and hence had at its disposal a formidable proportion of the state administration-controlled economic resources.

But the religious parties, when they participated in the government coalition, also obtained their share. The ultra-Orthodox party Agudat Israel left the coalition in the early 1950s, but the National Religious Party (NRP) (previously the Mizrahi and Hapoel Hamizarahi parties) was Mapai's almost constant coalition partner. It had several ministries under its control, and used these – and the resources of which these ministries had charge – to channel funds to various institutions connected to it, to contribute religious articles to congregations, and to hand out jobs and financial aid to actual and potential supporters.

In this manner, party-linked, but state-financed, institutions once more provided the necessities for people's lives, in return for their support at the ballot box.

THE PERPETUATION OF THE SYSTEM

In the 1970s the politicization of the state bureaucracy was curbed to some extent. But in 1977 there was a changeover of government whereby, for the first time, the right-wing Likud Party came to power. This, once more, led to the subordination of administrative power to politics.

While they were still in opposition, the leaders of the Likud had vociferously criticized the practice. Hence, it could have been expected that when they came to power, they would abolish it. And, indeed, at the beginning of the Likud era, party-political appointments in the state administration declined.

Gradually, however, the practice was reinstated. The religious parties were especially successful in this respect. While the Labour Alignment

Party (previously Mapai) and the Likud had changed places in government, the religious parties were the coalition partners of both sides. The NRP remained in the coalition, Agudat Israel rejoined it, and newly created religious parties, in particular the ultra-Orthodox Shomrei Tora Sfaradim (Shas), followed suit. A tradition developed whereby certain ministries (such as those of the interior and of religious affairs) remained almost permanently in the religious parties' domain, and appointments in these ministries were such as to give preference to those parties' supporters, as a matter of course.

In this manner, the system was perpetuated into the 1980s, and into the beginning of the 1990s. By the testimony of Professor Amnon Rubinstein, a Knesset member who subsequently became a government minister,[7] the practice at the end of the 1980s, no less than previously, was for government ministers to implant their party faithful into the civil service. Since previous government implants held tenure, they were not dismissed. But frequently they were moved aside and disregarded, and often they remained without any real jobs to perform.

Another testimony to the perpetuation of the system at the end of the 1980s, may be found in the State Comptroller's Office (SCO) reports of the years 1989 and 1990.[8] According to these, political appointments were widespread in all parts and all ranks of the state administration. Sometimes appointments were made without advertisement of the positions. At other times, formally correct appointment procedures were observed, but a closer examination of the appointments showed that the candidates were in fact selected on the basis of their political connections. Also, promotions of political appointees proceeded at a faster pace than those of other appointees.

All this was reflected in the manner in which state resources were distributed to the public. In the 1970s, when political appointments in the civil service declined to some extent, and the power of the administrative elite gained a degree of autonomy from politics, the handing out of benefits by political criteria abated as well.

These years were characterized by a process of the depillarization of political parties, and a decrease in their ability to take charge of people's lives. By that time, the immigrants of the 1950s had established themselves, and their dependence on party-linked absorbing agencies declined. Then, too, various spheres of activity, which had previously been in the hands of political parties and the Histadrut, were transferred to government departments which, by then, were less politicized than they had been in the past. So, various goods and services (such as benefits for housing) were now meted out to the public by criteria of need and entitlement, rather than by partisan considerations.

Under Likud rule, however, the renewed subjugation of administrative power to government political power was reflected in the allocation of such goods and services, albeit only to parts of the public. Two intermeshed patterns of politically motivated allocations became prominent: the flow of funds through a government ministry via local authorities, and the flow of 'special' funds through government ministries directly to their targets. In both cases, institutions linked mainly to the religious parties were the chief beneficiaries. Neither pattern could have come into being without the administration's being accommodating to government politicians.

THE FLOW OF FUNDS THROUGH LOCAL AUTHORITIES

This flow took place from the Ministry of the Interior to local authorities, and therefrom, to institutions and associations connected to the particular religious party that held sway over the Ministry of the Interior at that particular time. During the years in which the ministry was in the hands of the NRP, large-scale funds were channelled into institutions connected to that party. In more recent years, when this ministry was under the aegis of Shas, the bodies linked to that party became the main beneficiaries.

These included the Shas-linked educational network El Hama'ayan (To the Spring), mikvaot (ritual baths), synagogues and more. During the years 1987–89 alone some 90 million shekels were channelled through municipalities in this manner, and at that time, this sum was worth much more than it would be today. In 1982, the director general of the Ministry of the Interior published guidelines for the distribution of funds through local authorities, whereby this distribution by political criteria was to be curbed. In 1985 an interdepartmental committee published formal rules and guidelines for the allocation of such funds.[9] Nevertheless, the transfer of funds from the Ministry of the Interior through the local authorities for political purposes continued. This was so, even though this allocation was irregular, and in contravention to the formal rules, drawn up by the top echelon of the ministry itself.

The SCO report of 1991 uncovered the fact that, despite these formal rules and guidelines, the allocation of funds to party-linked institutions reached unprecedented dimensions when the Ministry of the Interior was under Shas domination.[10] The allocations were designed to entice the many beneficiaries of these institutions and associations – directors, teachers, administrators, other employees, religious functionaries, clients and parishioners – to support the party, by reason of the generosity from which they benefited. Indirect evidence for this may be found in the fact that in 1988, an election year, these allocations increased by 170 per cent, while the consumer price index rose by 17.4 per cent only. And since the various beneficiaries of the party-linked bodies could continue to gain those benefits only if the party's electoral power enabled it to take charge of the Ministry of the Interior once more after the election, it was in their interest to increase this party's electoral success by voting for it.

One explanation for the willingness of local authorities to serve as an intermediary for the flow of political funds may be found in their dependence on the Ministry of the Interior for their own funds. This made it difficult for them to decline its requests. But the flow of funds could not have taken place were it not for an additional factor: the party politicization of the civil service in the Ministry of the Interior. Had this not been the case, senior administrators would have been likely to follow the clear-cut, formal rules set out by the ministry itself, which prohibited such transfers of funds for political purposes. Only the political allegiance of these administrators to the minister of the interior and his party explains their willingness to disregard the appropriate rules in the execution of the payments.

This allegiance explains in particular how it comes about – as the above-mentioned SCO reports clarified – that ostensibly separate institutions, that were discovered to have the same bank accounts, continued to draw double payments. The same allegiance also explains how it is that compliant municipalities, which were not entitled to certain fund allocations, nevertheless obtained them and, indeed, obtained more than they had applied for. In more general terms, the political dependence of the senior officials in the Ministry of the Interior explains why those of them who were in charge of fund allocation acted according to the instructions of politicians, even when these contravened the rules laid down by their own ministry.

THE FLOW OF 'SPECIAL' FUNDS

The second of the new patterns of resource allocation involves the flow of what came to be known as 'special' funding, which is but another name for politically motivated funding. The allocation of such funds was anchored in – overt or covert – coalition agreements, whereby the religious parties joined the government coalition, in return for such 'special' allocations being made to the institutions and associations specified by them.

At times, these funds reached their destination via individual Knesset members. At other times, they were channelled through government ministries. In either case, they ended up in the coffers of party-linked institutions and associations. In this, they were similar to monies that flowed through local authorities, except that in this case other ministries were involved, and they did not utilize the local authorities for the purpose at hand.

The 'special' funds were allocated, first and foremost, to religious educational institutions and other religious associations through the

Ministry of Education and the Ministry of Religious Affairs. The organizations that benefited were chiefly those connected to the ultra-Orthodox parties Agudat Israel, which later became Yahadut Hatora (Tora Jewry), and Shas. They included kindergartens, primary and secondary schools and yeshivot (colleges of higher religious education).

We may learn something on the dimensions of such funding from the testimony of Uzi Bar-Am who, for a brief spell, was minister for religious affairs, in the Labour government elected in 1992. According to his testimony,[11] on assuming office he found that out of the ministry's budget of 800 million shekels, 500 million had gone to party-linked religious bodies. To this must be added the funds that accrued to party-connected religious educational institutions through the Ministry of Education. All in all, in 1992, some 600 million shekels in 'special' funds went to religious party-allied organizations and associations.

As far back as 1983, the Knesset had passed a resolution whereby 'special' funds were to be allocated by objective criteria only. The Knesset further resolved that the ministries in charge of the allocations were to inspect the institutions that were their beneficiaries, to ensure that they met the criteria set out for the allocations.

Accordingly, the Ministry of Religious Affairs drew up regulations whereby to qualify for 'special' funding from it, an educational institution must have at least 25 registered students, and the absence of more than a quarter of these at the time of the inspection would lead to the cessation of payments. In May 1984 the High Court of Justice also ruled that 'special' allocations were to be granted only on the basis of objective criteria. This, however, is not what happened in practice.

According to the SCO reports of 1984 and 1985,[12] the Ministries of Education and of Religious Affairs continued to disregard even the most elementary rules of fund allocation. They did not require funded institutions to render account on the manner in which the monies were spent. Some of their students were registered simultaneously in different institutions. Checks on the number of students that were actually attending the funded institutions were rare; and when they took place, in some cases, as many as 60 per cent of the registered students were absent.[13]

In spite of this, no steps were taken to penalize such institutions. A former director general of the Ministry of Religious Affairs, in testimony before a special Knesset Committee in 1989, stated that several institutions enjoying political funding were in fact non-existent, while others were short-lived and had but minute numbers of students.

Like the funds via local authorities, the 'special' funding, too, was designed to serve as an enticement to tie the beneficiaries – employees and clients of the funded institutions – and their families to the parties that were their benefactors. This is evident from the fact that children in politically funded educational institutions enjoyed better conditions than pupils in other institutions. For instance, children in the Shas-sponsored 'El Hama'ayan' educational system (unlike children in regular schools) obtained hot meals, and were kept in school for longer hours. Yeshiva students (unlike university students) paid no tuition, unmarried ones obtained free boarding in their institutions, and married ones drew monthly allowances. The overall number of students in the 'special' institutions numbered tens of thousands of students, who all had parents and any number of siblings and other family members. Hence, the electoral support that the parties sponsoring such institutions could hope for was not negligible.

Like the allocation of funds through the municipalities, the 'special' funding arrangements could not have come about without the dependence of administrative power on political power, and without its employment in the service of party politics. A politically independent state bureaucracy could not have abolished the coalition agreements that stipulated such funding. But such an independent bureaucracy would have made the allocations in accordance with the rules and criteria, which their own ministries had set up, and which were subsequently disregarded.

Moreover, had the monies indeed been allocated according to the rules that called for objective criteria of need and entitlement, they would have lost their 'special' status. This means that they would have continued to flow to the institutions in question, even without the parties' patronage. Therefore, they could no longer have served to tie supporters to the parties.

Indeed, it is precisely the *absence* of proper criteria which made the 'special' funding contingent on the sponsoring party's electoral success and consequent political clout. So, only the irregularity of funding could motivate the beneficiaries to extend their electoral support to the party, in order to ensure the continuation of the funding. And it is precisely such irregularity, which an independent bureaucratic elite, acting according to objective, rather than political, criteria could have prevented.

RECENT DEVELOPMENTS

In recent years, some attempts have been made to reform the state administration, so as to render it more autonomous from politics – but to no avail. Most prominently, an attempt to institute such a reform was made in the years 1994 through 1996, by the then civil service commissioner. One of its central aims was to depoliticize the public administration, or at least to establish clear boundaries for political involvement.

On the initiative of the civil service commissioner, in 1994 the cabinet appointed a special committee charged with the task of recommending new criteria for political appointments in the civil service. In 1995, the committee submitted its recommendations, which were that henceforward, political appointments in the civil service were to be reduced, and confined to national policy positions only. No political appointments or political intervention would be allowed below the level of director general. Incoming ministers would be allowed to appoint a small staff of advisers and aides, but these would serve on a temporary basis, and come and go with their ministers.

However, these recommendations did not gain sufficient government support. Especially with the subsequent changeover of government in 1996, the depoliticization of the civil service was halted, and the goal of redefining the relationship between the political and the administrative elites was frustrated.[14]

At that time, the civil service commissioner was replaced, and the Civil Service Commission was transferred from the Ministry of Finance to the Prime Minister's Office. This made it easier to circumvent the regulations limiting political appointments in the state administration. It was thus a step towards the further subordination of administrative to political power.

Most recently, the partisan hegemony over government ministries has persisted, and top administrative appointments have still been political. Consequently, senior officials have remained loyal not only to the party under whose auspices they were appointed, but also to the factions and ministers responsible for these appointments. Thus, the state administration has not gained professional autonomy, and has remained greatly responsive to the politicians in charge.[15]

All this remained salient first and foremost on the higher rungs of the administrative ladder, but it is here that the bulk of administrative power is concentrated. Moreover, even recently, political appointments have not been confined to this level only. According to the testimony of a senior aide to the late prime minister Yitzhak Rabin,[16] in recent years political appointments have encompassed thousands of jobs at all levels.

This has been most clearly evident in the ministries allocated to the smaller coalition parties, particularly the religious ones, such as the Ministry of the Interior, the Ministry of Religious Affairs and the Ministry of Education. But it has by no means been confined to them. In the Ministry of Communications, which during the years 1996–99 was in the hands of the Likud, dozens of Likud activists were appointed to civil service positions. In addition, the Likud minister for communications was in charge of various statutory bodies, such as the post office, and the telephone company, Bezek. In each of these bodies political appointments abounded.

Since the Labour Party was in opposition during 1996–99 it had no ministries in which to make political appointments. Following the May

1999 election, the party – later the chief component of the movement named 'One Israel' – was again voted into office. As could have been expected on the basis of its previous record, in this new guise, too, it continued the time-honoured practice of the politicization of the state bureaucracy.

Up until recently, it was customary for the most senior civil service appointments to be made without the positions being advertised. In October 1998, following a ruling of the High Court of Justice, the civil service commissioner announced that henceforward virtually all positions (with very few exceptions) would have to be advertised. However, politicians (of whatever parties) in charge of ministries found ways of circumventing or bending this rule, as they have done in the past. Moreover, experience has shown that since the advertising of positions may be manipulated, this cannot prevent the political appointment of previously selected candidates.

ADMINISTRATIVE POWER AND THE PARTIES' ELECTORAL BODIES

There is one peculiar connection between administrative power and politics that has become especially salient in recent years. This is the appointment of members of the party's central committee, or the delegates to the party's congress, to senior positions in the civil service.

This practice developed because of the prominent role such bodies have assumed in recent Israeli politics. In several parties, including the Likud, the central committee assumed the role of electing the party's candidates for the Knesset. In the Labour Party, the delegates to the party's congress fulfilled this task. Also, if one or the other of the parties subsequently came to power, those candidates who gained the largest numbers of votes in their parties' respective electoral bodies stood a good chance of being selected for ministerial positions.

Therefore, it has been expedient for politicians with ministerial ambitions to muster support for themselves in their parties' electoral bodies. And it became customary for them to do so by promising members of those bodies that, if they became ministers, they would appoint them to senior administrative positions, in return for their votes. Once elected and entering the government, the ministers in fact discharged their previously incurred obligations by making the promised political appointments. The political appointees in the civil service then reciprocated, by once more voting for the ministers who appointed them, in the subsequent internal party elections for the party's candidates to the next Knesset and the next government.

Professor Amnon Rubinstein, who in 1990 was a member of the Knesset (and later became a government minister) summarized the situation in a submission to the Knesset, in which he wrote: 'One of the

worst aspects of the politicization of the civil service, is the appointment
of certain people, for no other reason than their being members of the
central committee of the party of the minister, in whose ministry the
appointment is being made'.[17]

In February 1992, when the Likud was in office, the then civil service
commissioner published an estimate whereby, at the time, there were no
fewer than 252 members of the Likud's central committee, who also held
senior positions in the state administration. In the run-up to the 1992
election, both the Likud and the Labour Party introduced primaries, in
which candidates for the Knesset (and hence for the government) were
elected by all registered members of the party. In the 1996 election, the new
system of the direct popular election of the prime minister was introduced.
At that time, the parties' candidates for the Knesset as well as for the prime
ministership – in both Labour and the Likud – were elected by registered
party members in primaries, and the parties' central committee and congress
respectively thus lost much of their erstwhile power.

Prior to the 1999 election, however, this decision was reversed. While
the candidates for the prime ministership in both the Labour Party and the
Likud continued to be elected in primaries, the election of candidates for
the Knesset (and thus for ministerial positions) was once again vested in
the parties' electoral bodies (the central committee in case of the Likud,
and the party convention in case of the Labour Party). These bodies thus
regained their previous power, and candidates for the Knesset once again
mustered support for themselves in those bodies, by promising their
members administrative positions, in return for their votes.

At present, the law bars civil servants who are also members of parties'
electoral bodies from participating in the internal party elections held in
those bodies. Nevertheless, before the 1999 election, scores of civil
servants participated in such elections in their parties' electoral bodies, of
which they were members. It was virtually impossible for the civil service
commissioner to track down all politically appointed civil servants who
had transgressed the law in this manner.

Moreover, even if members of the said electoral bodies upheld the law,
and did not participate in the elections held in these bodies, the fact
remained that they were the ministers' appointees, hence under an
obligation to promote their ministers' political interests.

FROM 'SPECIAL' FUNDING TO 'SPECIAL' CRITERIA

In view of all this, it is not surprising that the state bureaucracy is still
being used for the flow of party patronage.

In 1992 the Knesset passed a law, which officially abolishes 'special'
funding for party-linked institutions and associations. The law provides
that, henceforward, state allocations of funds through the various

ministries are not to be made to individual bodies, but are to be executed by general, objective, equitable criteria, to be set up by these ministries.

It soon became apparent, however, that this attempt at transformation of the system, too, has failed. The provisions of the law to set up criteria for fund allocations have been upheld, but the criteria came to be manipulated to suit the convenience of politicians. Indeed, institutions and associations that were previously politically funded began to draw even larger funds than they did before.[18] Thus, instead of 'special' funding, we now have 'special' criteria, which serve the same purpose.

The situation did not remain entirely static over the years. During the years 1992–96, when Labour was in office, the NRP did not join the government coalition. Thus it lost the Ministries of Education and Religious Affairs – that had frequently been in its domain – and the flow of funds thereto appertaining. The ultra-Orthodox parties Yahadut Hatora and Shas did not join the government coalition either, but they demanded – and obtained – additional funding for their institutions, whenever an important issue came up for a vote in the Knesset, for which the government required their support.

With the inauguration of the Likud government in 1996, all the religious parties once again joined the government coalition, and the flow of funds to their respective institutions and associations once again flourished. And, as before, the channelling of funds again took place through the various ministries of which the religious parties were in charge, chiefly the Ministries of Education, of Religious Affairs, and of Labour and Welfare. And, once again, this was done with the connivance of the politically appointed civil servants in these ministries.

The system has not only been partisan, but in many cases has verged on corruption or beyond. Frequently, the institutions and associations that obtained political funding were not held accountable on how they spent the monies. Also, several of them existed on paper only, and could not be located at their registered addresses. Some of them obtained funding from more than one ministry at one and the same time.

Thus, as before, the SCO report of 1995 once more revealed that the Ministry for Religious Affairs, which previously had been under Shas control, continued to distribute monies to institutions on the basis of false reports.[19] It did so without any real inspection of these institutions, and giving special preference to those that were linked to Shas. The SCO report further revealed that the same practice was followed under the Labour government, after Shas had seceded from the government coalition, and the Ministry of Religious Affairs had passed into the hands of the Labour Party. Towards the end of Labour's term of office, some reforms of the system were beginning to be introduced,[20] but then the 1996 election brought the Likud to power, and the previous trends once more gained momentum.

According to the SCO report of 1999,[21] despite a 1997 ruling of the High Court of Justice prohibiting this, hundreds of institutions and associations continued to obtain financial support from two or more ministries, in particular the Ministries of Education, of Religious Affairs and of Labour and Welfare.

Also, according to this report, at the beginning of 1998, all institutions obtaining funding from the Ministry of Religious Affairs were required to report on the numbers of their students. The institutions were also required to employ auditors, to make separate reports on the numbers of their students. Of the approximately 2,300 institutions obtaining funding from the Ministry of Religious Affairs, in 1,250 there were significant differences between the numbers of students reported by the institutions and the numbers of students reported by the institutions' internal auditors.

In addition, the State Comptroller's Office itself engaged some independent auditors to check on the numbers of students in parts of these same institutions. These checks revealed that the numbers of students claimed by the institutions, and even the number of students claimed to exist by the institutions' internal auditors, greatly exceeded the number of students actually present, when the *independent* auditors' inspections took place. On top of this, some 260 institutions did not even bother to submit the required reports on the numbers of their students.

In line with this, a special investigation carried out by the newspaper *Yediot Ah'ronot* revealed that, in recent years, billions of shekels have been distributed by the Ministry of Religious Affairs in this manner.[22] And according to the SCO report of 1999, some 181,000 yeshiva students (and their families) benefited from them.[23]

THE MACHINATIONS OF THE SYSTEM

How does the system work? Usually it is the minister himself who sets out the criteria for the allocations. In each ministry, the actual allocations are made by committees composed of the ministry's auditor general, its legal adviser and various senior civil servants, almost all of whom are the minister's appointees, and his political allies and party faithful.

Moreover, there are no independent bodies that effectively oversee and control the allocations. Formally, the registrar of associations is in charge of doing so. In fact, however, he is incapable of carrying out the task, because of understaffing and lack of powers of enforcement. The State Comptroller's Office, because of its small staff, can do no more than examine a few of the thousands of bodies that obtain political funding each year.

In practice, the only authority that can hold these organizations accountable for the manner in which they operate (or fail to operate), and for the manner in which they spend the monies allocated to them, is the same ministry, whose senior civil servants are the political appointees of the minister, and who have made the allocations in the first place.

CONCLUSION

Administrative power in Israel has worked in the service of politics right from the beginning, and up until this day. Nevertheless, there have been some changes in this respect. During the pre-state era and at the beginning of statehood, this system benefited first and foremost the main party that was in power, Mapai. And only in the second place did it work in the interest of the other labour parties and the religious parties.

Since the 1970s, when the right-wing Likud first came to power – and subsequently the Likud and Labour periodically replaced each other in office – the main beneficiaries of the system have been the religious parties, and in particular the ultra-Orthodox parties Yahadut Hatora (previously Agudat Yisrael) and Shas.

In recent years, whenever they have been in office, the Likud and the Labour Party too have been able to stack parts of the state administration with their supporters. But, unlike the religious parties, they have not have had a substantial success in utilizing their footholds in the administration for the purpose of handing out material benefits to large numbers of their potential supporters. Thus, unlike Mapai of previous years, and unlike the religious parties in later years, recently these two parties have not been successful in translating the administrative power subservient to it into a major electoral asset.

The politicization of administrative power has never been the sole determinant of the outcome of elections. The parties have always differed from each other in their ideologies, and the personalities of their leaders have also been of great importance in influencing people's votes, as have been the voters' religious versus secular allegiances. Nevertheless, the electoral manipulation made possible by the politicization of the civil service has also been of considerable importance. It has certainly contributed to the situation whereby Mapai, later the Labour Party, was in office from the early 1930s (in the pre-state National Institutions) up until the late 1970s.

Today, too, the utilization of parts of the administration for partisan purposes does not determine the outcome of elections, but it does exert a certain influence on them. This is so, especially as far as the two ultra-Orthodox parties are concerned, a large part of whose voters obtain party-channelled benefits. These voters stand to incur major material losses if their parties lose much of their electoral power, and cease to be attractive coalition partners to whatever party happens to be in office. Hence, such administration-channelled material benefits serve as a major factor in motivating the voters of the ultra-Orthodox parties to extend their allegiance to them.

This is so particularly in the case of Shas. For while the Yahadut Hatora voters are generally ultra-Orthodox themselves, and probably would have supported this party in any case, this is not so for Shas. This party has been able to marshal support also among many people who are not Orthodox, but merely traditional. These are generally people who originate from Middle Eastern countries, who are of relatively lower socio-economic background, and stand in need of the benefits, which Shas has been able to provide for them and their children. And many of these tend to vote for Shas chiefly for the sake of these administration-channelled benefits. Indeed, this may be one major explanation for Shas's phenomenal success in the 1999 election, in which it gained 17 seats in the Knesset.

All in all, the services which administrative power has rendered to politics have not destroyed Israeli democracy. Political battles among the parties have always been of major importance, and are still vigorously fought. And the personalities of the parties' leaders are still of great importance in shaping the public's electoral decisions. But the electoral manipulation brought about by administrative politicization has not been a negligible factor in determining electoral outcomes. Hence it has detracted from the quality of Israeli democracy. Certainly it has done nothing to promote its health.

NOTES

1. Max Weber, *The Theory of Social and Economic Organization*, trans. A.M. Henderson, New York: Free Press, 1947; Max Weber, *Economy and Society*, 3 vols, New York: Bedminster, 1968; Gaetano Mosca, *The Ruling Class*, trans. H.D. Kahn, New York: McGraw Hill, 1939; Joseph Schumpeter, *Capitalism, Socialism and Democracy*, 3rd edn, New York: Harper, 1962; Raymond Aron, *Progress and Disillusion*, London: Pall Mall, 1968; Eva Etzioni-Halevy, *Bureaucracy and Democracy: A Political Dilemma*, 2nd edn, London: Routledge & Kegan Paul, 1985; Eva Etzioni-Halevy, *The Elite Connection: Problems and Potential of Western Democracy*, Cambridge: Polity Press, 1993; Eva Etzioni-Halevy (ed.), *Classes and Elites in Democracy and Democratization*, New York: Garland Publishing, 1997.
2. Other elites include the business elite, the key people in the media, top-ranking military officers, trade union leaders, and more.
3. Eva Etzioni-Halevy, *The Elite Connection and Democracy in Israel*, Tel Aviv: Sifriat Poalim, 1993 (in Hebrew); Eva Etzioni-Halevy, *A Place at the Top: Elites and Elitism in Israel*, Tel Aviv: Tcherikover Publishers, 1997 (in Hebrew).
4. Ross E. Buckhart and Michael S. Lewis-Beck, 'Comparative Democracy: The Economic Development Thesis', *American Political Science Review*, Vol. 16 (1994), pp.903–10.
5. Eva Etzioni-Halevy, *Political Manipulation and Administrative Power: A Comparative Study*, London: Routledge & Kegan Paul, 1979.
6. Simha Werner, 'Ethics and Morality in the Public Administration: Towards the Third Generation', in Aharon Kfir and Yakov Reuveny (eds.), *Public Administration in Israel: Towards the 2000s*, Tel Aviv: Tcherikover Publishers, 1999, pp.131–65 (in Hebrew).
7. Amnon Rubinstein, 'Overcoming Political Appointments', *Ha'aretz*, 21 May 1989.

8. State Comptroller's Office, *Annual Report No. 34* and *Annual Report No. 35*, Jerusalem: State Comptroller's Office, 1984 and 1985.
9. Werner, 'Ethics and Morality', p.141.
10. State Comptroller's Office, *Annual Report No. 41*, Jerusalem: State Comptroller's Office, 1991.
11. Reported in *Ha'aretz*, 28 Dec. 1992.
12. State Comptroller's Office, *Annual Report No. 34* and *Annual Report No. 35*.
13. Etzioni-Halevy, *The Elite Conncection*, pp.75–6.
14. Yitzhak Galnoor, David Rosenbloom and Allon Yaroni, 'Creating New Public Management Reforms: Lessons from Israel', *Administration and Society*, Vol. 30 (1998), pp. 393–420.
15. Galnoor *et al.*, 'Creating New Public Management Reforms'.
16. Ethan Haber, 'Hollander's Finger in the Hole of the Dam', *Yediot Ah'ronot*, 8 Nov. 1998.
17. Uri Struman, 'An Overly Comprehensive Law', *Ha'aretz*, 4 March 1999.
18. Amnon De-Hartuch, 'State Support for Public Institutions: The Blooming of Special Funding', *Mishpatim*, Vol. 29 (1998), pp.109–37 (in Hebrew).
19. State Comptroller's Office, *Annual Report No. 45*, Jerusalem: State Comptroller's Office, 1995.
20. Werner, 'Ethics and Morality', p.142.
21. State Comptroller's Office, *Annual Report No. 49*, Jerusalem: State Comptroller's Office, 1999.
22. Galit Yemini, 'The Name of the Association', *Yediot Ah'ronot*, 15 Dec. 1998.
23. State Comptroller's Office, *Annual Report No. 49*.

The Functioning of Whatever Is the Israeli State

IRA SHARKANSKY

It is conventional to regard the functioning of public administration as reflecting the nature of governmental structure, as well as traits of the economy and society. What is distinctive about a country as it is compared to others is likely to affect how its government operates. The title of this article raises a question as well as providing a clue to the answer that a reader should expect to find. In Israel's case, several of its distinctive features render the state peculiar, as well as affecting the nature of public administration.

We must be careful. Israel's controversial history provokes numerous allegations of peculiarity that are not justified by comparison. We have no wish to quarrel with the concepts of 'Promised Land' and 'Chosen People' as interpreted by religious Jews, Christians and others, but these concepts are partly to blame for unjustified assertions about the special nature of the Israeli case. Local and international aspirations are high. Israelis and Israeli-watchers credit or accuse the society of accomplishments or faults to which it is not entitled.[1] Israel is not the best or the worst of countries. However, it does differ from numerous others in several traits that affect its public administration. Two of the most prominent among these traits are the concentration of its population in one part of the small country; and the dominant position of national ministries in the country's government and economy. Somewhat less obvious, but also distinctive, is the interpenetration of politics and public administration.

A METROPOLITAN CITY-STATE

'Metropolitan Israel' does not exist in any formal sense, but appears in the concentration of population, politics and policy-making activity in a triangle that extends along the coast for about 100 miles from Ashkelon in the south to Nahariya in the north, with a bulge in the centre 35 miles eastwards to Jerusalem. The area contains some 81 per cent of the

Ira Sharkansky is Professor of Political Science and Public Administration at the Hebrew University of Jerusalem.

national population, and 23 per cent of the land area, not counting occupied territories. Israel's metropolitan core is smaller than the metropolitan areas of Houston, Los Angeles and Seattle.[2]

Metropolitan Israel dominates a small country that is one of the most highly urbanized. Israel is two-thirds the size of Belgium. Ninety per cent of Israel's population lives in settlements of more than 2,000 residents, and 81 per cent in settlements of more than 10,000. Of 22 developed countries, only the United Kingdom has a higher incidence of urban population. Among American states, only California has a higher incidence of urban population.

Metropolitan Israel is the focus of a political culture and policy-making that are essentially national in character. Most Israeli families arrived in the country only during this century. Despite some claims of developing regional loyalties,[3] there are as yet no strong indications of sub-national attachments or accents. The mythic intention of the Zionist pioneers was to build a nation of farmers in order to set themselves apart from what they perceived as a historical distortion of the Jewish people as urban bourgeois. According to an Israeli sociologist, however, they succeeded only in ignoring the urban-focused stream of immigration, and denying city planning of the talents it should have received during the period of nation-building.[4] Not acknowledged in the Zionist myths were the urban roots of the ancient Judeans as well as the urban patterns of Jewish settlement in the Diasporas prior to the creation of modern Israel. Jerusalem was the urban centre of the faith and the locale of many events described in the Hebrew Bible.

The Knesset is elected on the basis of proportional representation from a single national constituency. Although the major parties make some effort to include representatives of key localities and regions on their lists of candidates, most national figures identify with the cities of Jerusalem or Tel Aviv, or their immediate surroundings. The mayors of Jerusalem and Tel Aviv have been leading figures in one or another of the two major political parties, and provide access for their local needs to national policy-makers. Daily newspapers and the electronic media are national in character, and come mostly from Tel Aviv or Jerusalem.

Arguably the dominant issues in Israeli policy are those which demand a national perspective. Defence and economic viability are perennially at the top of the agenda. The two issues are related, in so far as defence is unduly demanding of resources and helps to create a fragile economy. The international balance of trade is chronically negative. Annual inflation was between 100 and 400 per cent during the early 1980s. Recent Israeli inflation in the range of 4–5 per cent is two to three times the rates in the United States, Germany or Japan.

Migration is another issue with a national focus. Massive immigration was a major issue from 1948 to 1955 when refugees from Europe and the

Middle East more than doubled the population. Immigration spurted briefly in the early 1970s with a temporary opening of the Soviet Union, and became a major issue again from the late 1980s with the opening of Ethiopia and the collapse of the Soviet Union. The recent immigration is approaching one million and has added more than 15 per cent to the national population. The costs of transportation, housing, job creation and social services for immigrants fall largely on national ministries and quasi-government agencies.

Israel shares with numerous other countries complaints about excessive power in the hands of national government officials, and reform proposals in behalf of greater autonomy for local authorities. Alongside the concern for insufficient local autonomy there are also assertions of too much local autonomy. As elsewhere, reformers call for the integration, coordination or cooperation among local authorities in metropolitan areas.

Both sets of assertions bear examination in view of conditions that render the country an anomaly on the international scene. Israel is not so much a country with cities, as one metropolitan area within the structure of a country. Rather than join the chorus of reformers from other countries who complain about insufficient local autonomy or inadequate coordination in metropolitan regions, Israelis should recognize that they have what reformers elsewhere can generally not achieve: national concern for local problems, and a substantial degree of metropolitan integration that comes as a result of a convergence between local and national politics.

The issue of metropolitan integration surfaces in Israel, especially in the Tel Aviv area that includes six municipalities in the 100,000–200,000 population range, four in the 50,000–100,000 range, as well as the Tel Aviv–Yafo central city with its 350,000 residents, and a number of smaller municipalities.[5] The region is not without inequalities of resources and social problems, or government activities poorly coordinated across municipal boundaries. However, the police force is national. National ministries play dominant roles in education, public transport, traffic control, housing, welfare and the financing of local government. National government bodies have a crucial say about issues of water supply and physical planning. Reformers criticize the national ministry of environmental protection for being weak by Western European and North American standards, but it is the strongest player in its field. In this context, problems of metropolitan governance are less pressing than where strong municipal roles in education, policing, road construction and traffic control, taxation, environmental control and water supply frustrate policy integration or equity across urban areas.

A STRONG CENTRAL GOVERNMENT?

The national government that purportedly runs this highly concentrated country is strong.[6] Or is it? The Israeli state qualifies for the designation 'giant' by virtue of its domination of the national economy as well as the weight of its military on its neighbours and in the lives of Israeli citizens. The government is cumbersome by virtue of the inelegance by which its institutions manage their power. The results are not all bad. Inelegance adds to opportunities for personal discretion and the humanity of the Israeli state even while it produces shortfalls from standards of service, quality and equity. The reasons for the inelegance are instructive in their own right. They suggest that vexatious problems can further the pursuit of moral subtlety. An intensity of self-criticism is part of the country's morality. The self-criticism also frustrates any simple judgement of this cumbersome giant.

Concerns about the strength of the Israeli state go back to its beginning. Like almost all the other new states created with the weakening of European colonialism after the Second World War, Israel began with commitments to socialism. Like other new states, the lack of resources in the private sector dictated centralized public institutions to marshal resources and build infrastructure. Israel had the additional motivations of Zionist theory (a strong state to protect the people who had suffered from two millennia of statelessness, plus a degree of socialism to protect the weak) and the Central and Eastern European models of strong states that guided the national founders. A major war and mass immigration added to the powers of the state, as well as a Diaspora that was willing to loan and donate money to the new state and national institutions closely integrated with it.

Recent data of the World Bank show that Israel has been at or close to the top among a group of Western democracies in the percentage of gross national product represented by central government activities.[7] Citizens depend on the state and closely related institutions for almost all of their education, health care and public transport. And as might be expected, the strong state makes serious demands on its citizens. Income tax rates of 50 per cent apply to monthly incomes at the equivalent of US$4,700; a value added tax of 17 per cent applies to virtually all consumer spending; there are special purchase taxes of more than 100 per cent applied to the value of automobiles and other major items; local property taxes and national social security taxes are also significant. Military service demands two or three years from most young women and men, and continued reserve duty that may exceed 30 days a year for men until their 40s or 50s.

The designation of Israel as a giant is likely to evoke scepticism or outright ridicule among those who know it well. The connotation of significant size is one problem. In *God Knows*, a novel about the biblical

David, Joseph Heller has his hero boast, 'I had taken a kingdom the size of Vermont and created an empire as large as the state of Maine!'[8] Modern Israel is even more modest. It is a bit larger than New Jersey and a bit smaller than Massachusetts, and less than a quarter the size of Maine.

The governing of Israel is confounded because the country is more than the population and institutions located in its territory. Diaspora Jews have contributed the equivalent of $800 million in recent years to Israeli organizations, and they do not hesitate to speak about the actions of the Israeli government. Major donors shape the programmes that they support, and may demand to be heard by the prime minister and other policy-makers. Those who contribute modest sums can choose from a wide range of options. Individual universities, museums, theatres, orchestras, hospitals and religious academies seek overseas support, alongside the more general campaigns of the United Jewish Appeal in the United States and the United Israel Appeal outside the United States. For donors suspicious of established fund-raising, there are alternative programmes that support Jewish–Arab interactions, shelters for battered women and children, religious freedom and environmental protection.

The power of Diaspora Jewry, especially in the United States, produces a widening of the Israeli political arena. Israeli politicians circulate among American Jews as well as the United States' executive and legislative branches to press their party's posture on items of mutual interest. Diaspora activists contribute funds to those Israeli political parties and other organizations that express their political sentiments. For many Diaspora Jews, the watershed between unquestioned support of Israeli policies and criticism was the war in Lebanon that began in 1982. A prominent item on the agenda of Diaspora opposition is a perceived lack of accommodation by Israel's governments (especially those led by Likud prime ministers) with respect to its neighbours or its own Arab residents. Another item is a perceived oppression of non-Orthodox Jews. Yet another item, and one that reflects the diversity of the Diaspora, is the alleged failure of the Israeli government – even one led by a Likud prime minister – to do enough to ensure continued Jewish control of the land of Israel. While some wealthy overseas Jews support programmes meant to be accommodating with respect to Palestinians, other wealthy overseas Jews finance the activities of religious and nationalist movements intent on settling Jews in Arab neighbourhoods of Jerusalem, as well as other areas of the territories occupied in the 1967 war not yet turned over to the Palestinians.

POLITICS IN ADMINISTRATION: TECHNOCRATS IN POLITICS

'Politics' should not be a naughty word for students of public policy or public administration. The term refers to how individuals in a democracy decide about difficult issues. Ideally, politics proceeds by persuasion and voting in national campaigns, the legislature, or committees of officials charged with formulating the rules by which programmes operate. Politics also appears in staffing. Elected officials have a legitimate interest in filling key positions with individuals loyal to their policies. In this way, presumably, they advance the implementation of policies they were elected to support. Less admirable is the practice of filling numerous positions with friends, family members or party supporters, regardless of their professional qualifications.

For the most part, Western democracies have limited the extent of political appointments. Israel is among those countries which have established formal procedures designed to ensure the selection of the most qualified professionals available to its administrative positions. According to the State Service Law of 1959, positions may be filled only after the Civil Service Commission announces the opening and arranges a competitive selection.

What limit the working of the State Service Law are provisions for exempting positions from its coverage. Over the years a large number of slots have won these approved exemptions. In recent years, upwards of 25 per cent of appointments have been made to positions exempted from competitive selection.[9] Along with appointments that have been formally exempted from competitive selection, others have been defined as 'temporary', or have been filled by 'personal contract'. Some of these positions carry obvious sensitivity, as in the case of aides to the prime minister. And while some of these appointments have gone to individuals with professional qualifications, the evasions of competitive selection are open to political exploitation. Repeated inquiries of the State Comptroller's Office have cited ministers for manipulating the selection process in order to appoint their political supporters, often without the occupational qualifications supposedly demanded by the positions.[10]

The other side of the phenomenon labelled 'politicized administration' is electoral politics being taken over by upwardly mobile technocrats. The condition is most pronounced in the case of senior officers in the military or security services who become known among key politicians and the public during their professional careers, and are co-opted by the parties when they retire from the service to run for the Knesset or city halls. The most successful work their way to the pinnacle of national politics. Among the internationally known elected policy-makers with long prior experience in administrative positions are prime ministers Yitzhak Rabin, Shimon Peres, Yitzhak Shamir, Ehud Barak; mayors Teddy Kollek (Jerusalem), Shlomo Lahat (Tel Aviv), Amram Mitzna (Haifa); as well as present or former ministers of agriculture, labour, foreign affairs, health, infrastructure, internal security and defence.

HOW GOVERNMENT FUNCTIONS: FORMAL STRUCTURES AND RULES NEED NOT INDICATE WHAT REALLY OCCURS

The appointment of civil servants is not the only process where the formal rules provide an imperfect description of how Israeli government functions. The tight centralization that is formally a part of the Israeli regime is loosened in practice. A prominent theme of Israeli political science emphasizes the opportunities for local and even sub-local influence that fit within the formal rules of strict centralization.[11] The rules require the approval of each local authority's budget outlays by the Interior Ministry. The Education Ministry has substantial powers over curricula, and may approve or reject local proposals for the enrolment boundaries of each primary school. The Transportation Ministry must approve a municipality's recommendations to define streets as one-way or two-way, place traffic signs, and determine sites and regulations for vehicle parking. The Ministry of Housing and Construction is a dominant actor in the design and construction of new neighbourhoods and the refurbishing of older sites. In practice, each of these controls can bend to the political weight of local authorities, as well as the lack of ministerial resources to do what is necessary to carry out all that is required in order to exercise their powers.

Important for the informal rules of Israeli policy-making are political conditions at the national level. No political party has ever won a majority of the votes in an election for the Knesset. Leading parties have had to put together coalition governments with ministries passed out among the partners according to the number of seats they control in the parliament. Prime ministers have been unable to impose their will on the partners, except with respect to a few key issues in the coalition agreement. Issues of local government and other domestic policies have been lower on the list of priorities than defence and economic security. Individual ministers have been free to operate without having to concern themselves with integrated national policies.

Working in favour of clever municipal officials are the separate relations between local authorities and ministries that make expenditures on their own programmes in the local communities as well as provide funds to local authorities for specific programmes. The Interior Ministry provides a general grant for support of local activities. The Ministry of Housing and Construction pays for the construction of housing and roads. The Ministry of Religious Affairs supports synagogues, ritual baths, churches and mosques. The Ministry of Defence pays part of the costs of local civil defence. The Ministry of Health supports hospitals and local clinics. The Ministries of Education and Culture provide funds for local schools and cultural events. With the onset of substantial immigration from Ethiopia and the former Soviet Union, the Ministry of Immigration

Absorption became an important source of funds for social services. Researchers have commented on the problems in sorting through many years' worth of legislation, committee recommendations, court decisions, administrative rules, ministerial rulings and financial records in order to identify the major lines of policy pursued by national authorities. In many of the rules and regulations, there are provisions for ministerial discretion. The ministries may not move together in response to the same policy themes. Mayors have offered national politicians the opportunity to be the patrons of local projects. Ministers seek to advance their own reputations by favouring projects in local areas, whether or not they are not supported by the Ministries of Finance or Interior.

Officials are aggressive players in an intergovernmental game that is something of a free-for-all among contending authorities concerned to guard their powers or stretch the resources at their disposal. National ministries send inspectors to schools, welfare offices and other activities that they support, but there are not enough inspectors to keep tabs on local authorities. The Interior Ministry cannot keep to the formal schedule of reviewing local authority budgets. The formal approval required of each local authority's budget by the Interior Ministry is likely to come *after the end of the fiscal year, when a local authority's budget has been spent!* Local authority income is said to be fixed by nationally approved rates of taxation and service charges, but local authorities may ignore the bottom line on the budgets approved by the Interior Ministry. They transfer allocations from one item to another and run up sizeable indebtedness. Some have persuaded local banks to loan them money in violation of formal regulations, on the argument that the Finance Ministry will not allow local authorities to default on their obligations. Ministers and senior civil servants withhold payments or approvals for local projects in order to force a municipality's compliance with a ministry ruling, or to punish a municipality for overstepping its discretion. When a local authority reaches the end of its financial tether, it may suspend payment of salaries. Workers strike, street-side rubbish bins overflow, the public protests, the local authority complains that it cannot survive with existing allocations from the national government, Interior and Finance Ministries demand reductions in local authority budgets and workforces. Each side may make the appearance of giving in. Much occurs behind the scenes, with only the occasional story made available through the media or from insiders.

Jerusalem and Tel Aviv benefit from special treatment in the rough and tumble of Israeli public finance. Jerusalem receives an allocation from the national government for being the capital. The mayor and ranking municipal administrators argue in national ministries that extra budget allocations for housing and public facilities are necessary to improve the city's standing as the nation's showcase, to attract Jewish residents or to persuade Jews to remain in Jerusalem. At various times there has been a Cabinet Committee on Jerusalem or a Ministry of Jerusalem. While neither has had significant operational responsibility, they symbolize the concern of national policy-makers for the city and its continued status as Israel's capital. Tel Aviv pursues special resources on account of being the commercial and transportation hub of the country and the need to support public services that serve many non-residents. The mayors of both Jerusalem and Tel Aviv created non-governmental foundations that raise money from overseas donors for the construction of theatres, museums, parks and other public facilities, as well as for social services and cultural programming. The mayors have used those funds to prise matching resources from national ministries, and have gone to key donors with the prospects of putting their family name on projects that will be funded partly with government money.

Autocratic officials appear in local settings with a frequency not clearly less than their counterparts appear in national ministries. The local versions of arrogant bureaucrats provide one warning to reformers who expect that the quality of governance will clearly improve with more local autonomy. There is no obvious measure of governmental responsiveness that can be used to judge local or national personnel. Televised demonstrations of municipal and national politicians screaming at one another do not bode well for those who expect higher quality governance at the local level. School principals have tried to preserve smaller than average class sizes by telling newcomers to the neighbourhood that there is no room for their children. Such tricks may work on timid parents, but many Israeli citizens have learned that they must inform themselves of their legal rights and insist on them against officials who would serve their own organizations rather than the public. There are occasional reports of citizens who pass through insistence to shouting and then upsetting the office furniture in pursuit of their interests, and lead the police to intervene.

Israeli government does not proceed without a great deal of criticism. Academics and publicists from Israel and abroad accuse officials of state crimes or related sins for the illegal occupation of territory, the repression of a conquered population, illegal detentions, torture, censoring the media and piracy. Others find evidence of great disparities in the opportunities available to rich and poor, Jews and non-Jews, Jews from European and non-European backgrounds, men and women.[12]

The State Comptroller's Office is less flamboyant than university intellectuals or journalists in its criticisms of Israeli government, but must be counted among the prominent voices raised in condemnation. Like its equivalent audit bodies in other countries, the State Comptroller's Office cites public organizations for activities that are illegal, inefficient or ineffective. Unlike its counterparts elsewhere, the State Comptroller's

Office is authorized to criticize public bodies for failures of 'moral integrity'. The concern with moral integrity reminds us that Israel's auditor works in the same city as biblical prophets who criticized officials and economic elites for their lack of righteousness. Activities can be technically legal, but not good enough. The language of some reports concerned with moral integrity recall the language of the prophet Amos: 'Though ye offer me burnt offerings and your meat offerings, I will not accept them: neither will I regard the peace offerings of your fat beasts. Take thou away from me the noise of thy songs; for I will not hear the melody of thy viols. But let judgement run down as waters, and righteousness as a mighty stream.'[13]

Audit reports have targeted sensitive issues such as the handling of Arabs suspected of terrorism by the police, the allocation of resources to Arab education, and the quality of gas masks distributed to the public prior to the 1991 Gulf War.[14] Several reports have named leading political figures for handing out personnel appointments and purchase contracts in order to strengthen their party or their personal standing. One report sought to determine which of three public figures had lied about a politically sensitive subject. Another departed from the audit tradition of criticizing the activities of public officials and cited private citizens for what was perceived to be improper political activity. It listed 17 individuals or families who contributed more than NIS23,000 to each of two parties, and two individuals who contributed that sum to each of three parties. The contributions were not illegal, but the state comptroller felt that they were wrong. According to the report, 'Contributions to a party are meant to express support for the ideology and the program of the party. The giving of contributions to a number of parties by one contributor, even to parties of different ideologies, arouses wonder concerning the purpose of the contributor.'[15]

One of the contributors appeared on television to defend his legal and moral rights, and to question the state comptroller's right to criticize him. In an election that seemed to be closely contested, he wanted to assure post-election access for his points of view.

The state comptroller has paid a price for involvement in politically sensitive issues and personalities. Prime Ministers Yitzhak Shamir and Yitzhak Rabin responded with comments such as, 'Who is the state comptroller?' and 'Who is she anyway that she should squawk ...?' when programmes they supported were the targets of adverse audit reports. An ultra-Orthodox rabbi called the state comptroller 'wicked and an enemy of religion' in response to an audit report about a programme associated with his congregation.[16] As State Comptroller Miriam Ben Porat reached the end of her service she made two requests of the Knesset: (1) to give her a special term extension of three months, overlapping with the new comptroller, to complete certain investigations already under way, and (2) to approve cash payments for her accrued sick leave. A payment for sick leave not used is provided for other state employees, but not specifically for the comptroller. Both requests were denied. Newspaper reports and insider comments indicate that Knesset members responded to the requests with a correct but cool attitude. Some expressed wonder that she should even ask. In what may have been another response to the aggressive auditing by the State Comptroller's Office under Ben Porat, the Knesset appointed retired Supreme Court justice Eliezer Goldberg to be her replacement. Thus far he has shown little of the media-attracting personal style and politically sensitive reports of Miriam Ben Porat.

COPING IN THE FACE OF VEXATIOUS PROBLEMS

Israel would appear to qualify among the leaders in any contest to name countries beset with difficult matters. The list features numerous wars and countless attacks of terror; a developing economy strained by the costs of security and the absorption of several massive waves of needy immigrants; tensions between religious and secular Jews, between Jews of different national origins, and between Jews and Arabs; unfinished negotiations with Syria, Lebanon and Palestinians; as well as the especially sensitive problems of Jerusalem concerned with ethnicity and religion.

Coping is prominent in Israel's policy-making, and it seems more appropriate to its exasperating problems than any aspirations to solve them once and for all time. The synonyms of coping show that it seeks to manage difficulties rather than solve them:[17] *adapting, dealing with* and *satisfying*. These imply decisions that are 'good enough', even if they are not what any of the participants really want. Psychologists define coping as responses to stress, and have grouped coping behaviours in ways that are suggestive politically. Formulations for what some term 'active' and 'passive' coping are similar to what others call 'hardiness' and 'helplessness'. These concepts have their parallels in policy-making, where the terms *engagement* and *avoidance* are appropriate. Engagement (active coping) responds to stress with creativity, information-seeking, the re-definition and ranking of goals, seeking help and discipline. Avoidance (passive coping) is less constructive, and may be less successful in policy arenas. It responds to stress with a lack of control, hopelessness, confusion, rigidity, distortion, disorganization, randomness, disorder, distress, depression, anxiety, avoidance, withdrawal, flight or submission. It exhibits pointless emoting that involves loss of control and direction for oneself and potential allies; quixotic choice of options in an effort to *do something!* without taking account of likely costs and benefits; and frittering away resources in efforts that do not produce significant accomplishments.

Critics chastise the Israeli establishment for its failure to plan and formulate policy rationally, and to solve its problems. Another view is that coping reflects an acquired cultural capacity of Israeli Jews to deal at least partially with vexing problems.[18] Still pending is the question as to whether the coping skills that Jews learned as underdogs can be applied to a situation where Israeli Jews have greater power than minorities in their own country, and greater power than neighbouring countries.

ACCOMMODATION

Accommodation is a technique of coping. Its name suggests compromise, but accommodation can be more subtle. Accommodation in policy-making is not simply a division of the cake in equal shares. Accommodation seeks to keep the peace by anticipating demands, or reckoning with what it may take to keep a potentially antagonistic group at least minimally satisfied. It may give something even to those who are not currently making demands, entailing an accommodation to an adversary's perspective. Accommodation shows itself in Jerusalem, where the Arab minority has pointedly abstained from political activity in the Israeli municipality since 1967. Israeli authorities provided concessions that had not been formally requested by official Arab representatives in any established forum of government. They allowed Muslim religious leaders to remain in *de facto* control of holy sites also desired by Jews. They permitted Arab business and professional personnel to remain within existing Arab associations and the East Jerusalem Chamber of Commerce, rather than require them to obtain Israeli licences or to join Israeli associations that govern their members' practices. Israeli officials allowed Jordanian dinars to circulate in East Jerusalem, despite regulations that prohibited Israeli residents from dealing in foreign currency.

There is no assurance that accommodation will obtain the response that is intended. A beleaguered policy-maker may have to calculate how much of an accommodation will buy quiet from an adversary, and yet not cause allies to rebel against what they perceive as an excess of generosity. Israelis quarrel about the gestures made to Palestinians, with some taking the position that only force will produce peace.

AMBIGUITY

Ambiguity is a form of coping that serves as lubricant of politics.[19] Politicians make numerous promises that are far reaching in their implications, without specifying just what will be delivered. The deception can be intentional or innocent: associated with a politician who truly is Machiavellian, or an action by a politician who does not realize the implications of all the promises made for the sum of resources that will be available. Voters choose on the basis of generalized affection for a campaign. The successful politician can select among the commitments whose implementation can be reconciled with circumstances. It is a well-practised craft that reinforces a chronic cynicism about politicians, but generally does not threaten a regime. The appeal of ambiguity for a policy-maker is the opportunity to skip over especially contentious issues in the hopes that an 'understanding' will facilitate accommodation. Adversaries can reach agreement on the main outline of a programme without getting bogged down in all the messy details.

ILLUSTRATIONS AND DISCUSSION

Governance by coping is untidy and frustrating, but inevitable in settings beset with difficult problems and that truly are democratic. It is inherent in the ambiguity of politics that there are no clear boundaries between what should be permitted and forbidden, or between national purpose and legitimate self-interest.

Israel is not the only polity that illustrates these points. However, it provides sharply drawn examples in domestic and international relations. The words 'final solution' conjure up the ugly regime of the Nazis. They sought to rid the world of Jews, and killed some 40 per cent of those living in 1940. The record of the Nazis is one reason that Israeli politicians are disinclined to use the term final solution. Yet another reason might be their awareness that they are unlikely to resolve once and for all time the demands made by different groups of citizens.

JERUSALEM: ISRAELI AND/OR PALESTINIAN

While the problems focused on Jerusalem are widely thought to be the most difficult items on the Israeli–Palestinian agenda, the existing practice and future possibilities of ambiguity open possibilities that invite consideration. Elements of Israeli–Palestinian ambiguity have been in place since Israel expanded its presence as a result of the war of 1967, and the ambiguous character of Israeli–Palestinian relations in the city have developed further since the signing of the Oslo accords in 1993. Israeli and Palestinian authorities formally agreed on an absence of official Palestinian institutions in Jerusalem, but it is clear to all who read the Israeli press that Palestinian security forces operate in the city, that foreign dignitaries are received formally at the Palestinians' Orient House, that Palestinian authorities have a say about the operation of schools and hospitals formally administered by Israel, and that officials of the Palestinian Authority deal with constituent problems in Jerusalem.

Arabs living in East Jerusalem report problems among themselves to Palestinian authorities, and bring disputes to traditional Muslim courts for adjudication. A local newspaper headlined a report on Palestinian police activities in East Jerusalem with the claim that crime in the area was decreasing, while it was increasing in other areas of Israel. The article assigned credit to the Palestinian officers for East Jerusalem, in contrast with the disinclination of Israeli officials to serve the city's Palestinians.[20]

Despite more shrill calls for a totally Israeli administration in Jerusalem, Israeli authorities have looked the other way with respect to implementation. Hathem Abdel Kader, a member of the Palestinian Legislative Council, provoked one incident by receiving constituents in his Jerusalem home. To members of the Israeli cabinet, this was a step on the way to a Palestinian capital in Jerusalem. The Israeli minister of internal security reached an accord in which Kader said that he would not conduct business of the Palestinian Authority, per se, in Jerusalem. The 'policy' being followed seemed to resembled that of the United States military with respect to homosexuals: we won't ask; you don't tell.[21]

The most daring solution for Jerusalem is to avoid a solution! Both sides can consider the problem solved, and leave things more or less as they are. The Palestinians of East Jerusalem could continue complying with some Israeli regulations and receive Israeli social benefits, while continuing to resolve their internal problems with Muslim courts and Palestinian security personnel. Israel could insist that the city is united under its control as the capital of Jerusalem, while continuing to overlook the connections of Palestinians to another authority.

A realist can appreciate the appeal of such a non-solution, but doubt that it will satisfy. Neither Labour nor Likud politicians from the Israeli side, nor PLO leaders from the Palestinian side seems ready to describe in public the status quo or admit that it is satisfactory. Perhaps the essence of coping by way of ambiguity is just such an avoidance of truth. It works. But it may be able to continue only if it remains unarticulated.

A media flap in May 1998 revealed both the possibilities and problems of a finessed solution to the problems of Jerusalem. Israeli television broadcast pictures of a large structure being built alongside the boundary of the Jerusalem municipality. It took some days before Israeli authorities could agree that it was entirely outside their jurisdiction. According to initial reports, it was to be the parliament building of the Palestinian state. For some Israeli officials, it was ideal. The Palestinians could say that they had a capital in Jerusalem. Israel could accept the new fact, but would not have to concede the point. It was not in their Jerusalem. Right-wing activists boiled. The building proved the duplicity of Netanyahu. The building was closer to the Western Wall than was the Israeli Knesset. The prime minister was dividing Jerusalem.

Palestinians also had a problem with the building. Ardent nationalists saw it as betrayal. Arafat was agreeing on a capital only in the suburbs of

Jerusalem, and not in the city itself. Arafat waffled. PLO sources said that the building was not the parliament. It was a public facility. Perhaps a university. Then it was said to be for Arafat's offices.

The possibility exists that Israeli and Palestinian actions represent the further working out of ambiguous and tacit agreements. Ambiguity does not work if the parties make clear their intentions. To accept this bit of optimism, it is necessary to overlook the centrality and intensity of the 'Labour would divide Jerusalem' charge that the Likud featured in its electoral campaign of 1996 and repeated in the campaign of 1999, and the denials of those charges by Labour Party candidates. Perhaps the true situation is that some Israeli and Palestinian policy-makers are willing to cope with the benefits and problems of ambiguity, but others, or some of the same figures under the pressure of publicity, cannot depart from established slogans. With the onset of violence in 2000, accommodation and ambiguity seemed to have failed, at least for a while.

JUDAISM IN THE JEWISH STATE

Coping is also well established as a way for the Jews of Israel to deal with their own problems concerning the role of religion in public policy. Their agenda of dispute includes:

- Which aspects of religious law should be enforced by state authorities, and which bodies should have the final say in determining the nature of religious law and its application to individual cases? This cluster of issues includes the application of religious law to what is permitted on the Sabbath and religious holidays; the sale of non-kosher food; rules of modesty and decency; abortions, organ transplants and other medical practices; the treatment of ancient Jewish graves uncovered in construction projects; who should be considered a Jew; and who should be given the designation and authority of 'rabbi' to perform marriages, divorces and conversions to Judaism.
- What should be the rights and privileges of various categories of Jews? Religious and secular Jews, ultra-Orthodox, and non-Orthodox, as well as Jews from North Africa, Ethiopia and Asia feel that they have been treated unfairly by other Jews.
- The significance of the biblical land of Israel, and how much of that imprecise landscape should be insisted on, or bargained away for the sake of peace. Not the least of the issues in this cluster is Jerusalem, with its Jewish, Christian and Muslim holy places.

All of these controversies simmer without clear resolution. Individual cases get to the agenda, cause their commotion for days or weeks, and find some resolution. Before too long another issue emerges to reflect the same underlying disagreement.

In the case of the construction of roads and a new stadium that were opposed by religious activists on account of their causing violation of the Sabbath, the outcomes were delay or alteration in the implementation of policy rather than total reversal. One road project was delayed and its roadbed shifted slightly to avoid ancient graves discovered during excavations. The project then went forward despite additional graves located along the line of the new plans. A long-running conflict over a road through a religious neighbourhood in Jerusalem currently stands with the closure of the road during certain hours on Sabbath and religious holidays. This resolution is under appeal in the Supreme Court, but the Court seems in no hurry to decide the case.

The issue of 'indecent' advertising in bus stops has come to the public agenda several times with a wave of burning bus stops showing offensive posters, and then agreement between the advertising company and religious representatives. Laws prohibiting the sale of non-kosher food are not enforced. Non-observant Jews know which butcher shops sell pork under the label of 'white steak'. There is only sporadic enforcement of laws concerning the operation of businesses on the Sabbath.

Demands by non-Orthodox rabbis for recognition and funds for their congregations are viewed as challenges to the Orthodox religious establishment. The outcomes have been mixed. The status quo remains to provide Orthodox rabbis a monopoly of official functions with respect to marriages, divorces and conversions performed in Israel, but there has been an increase in the number of Reform and Conservative synagogues and schools, with financial support from government and quasi-governmental organizations. The Interior Ministry records marriages that occur outside Israel (sometimes arranged by mail) between individuals who could not be married by Israeli rabbis.

On the side of changes that reflect concessions to religious demands are the continued expansion of ultra-Orthodox neighbourhoods, and increased allocations of public resources to schools and other institutions of ultra-Orthodox communities. There is no lack of rhetoric surrounding these material benefits. Secular politicians charge that the religious parties inflate their demands and receive excessive material rewards by virtue of their importance in governing coalitions. Religious politicians insist that they operate according to the rules of Israeli politics, and continue to receive less than their fair share of resources. As in many other disputes involving religion, absolute truth eludes systematic research. Financial allocations for housing and infrastructure in religious neighbourhoods, and support for religious schools and other institutions come from a variety of ministerial and quasi-governmental budgets, under numerous programme headings, that may be kept ambiguous deliberately in order to prevent a final reckoning of *who gets what?*

On the side of clear secular victories is the opening of restaurants, discotheques and cinemas on the Sabbath. The municipal by-laws which had kept them closed were ruled to be flawed in a 1987 court decision, and religious politicians have not succeeded in enacting a new measure.

HIGH ASPIRATIONS AND FLAWED ACCOMPLISHMENTS

It is not only the most sensitive issues at the pinnacle of national and international interest that invite Israeli officials to operate with a casual regard for the formal rules. The condition may reflect habits learned while coping with issues of great complexity that encourage officials to act one way with respect to formal policy, but other ways informally. Issues of lesser prominence in government finance, land-use planning, environmental and safety regulations illustrate the point. Public officials routinely overrun their budgets. Land zoned for agriculture has been used for up-market housing and commercial development, at the considerable profit of moshavim and kibbutzim who sold their rights to the land. A deadly and embarrassing collapse of an ill-planned and sloppily constructed pedestrian bridge occurred during the opening ceremony of an international sports event. An impressive array of statutes and regulations supposedly dealing with water and air purity, safety regulations and solid waste disposal coexist with ugly and dangerous water courses, industries, fuel storage tanks and solid waste dumps within densely populated metropolitan areas.[22]

What unites all these cases is the impression of a country seeking to do too much with too little. The aspirations of Israelis to have a country ranking with the best have come up against Israel's limited resources, small space and congested population. Reformers aspiring to the best of policies in Western European and North America pass laws that lie dormant with minimum if any funding, staffing and implementation. The quotation attributed to the Zionist leader Theodore Herzl, 'If you wish it it will not be a legend' has come up against its limits. The Zionists have made a country, but alas it is limited.

THE STRESSFUL NATURE OF COPING

Coping does not only represent ways of dealing with serious problems. Coping also contributes stresses that add to the problems of policy-making. Israeli and Palestinian authorities, as well as ultra-religious and anti-religious Jews proclaim goals that are irreconcilable. Activists on all sides accuse their leaders of compromising basic aims. The conception of corruption may be blurred in a situation where sectoral interests with substantial public support push the limits of what is permitted. For almost a decade, Israel has been wrestling with the judicial and political significance of tactics pursued by Shas in order to fund its schools and other social institutions. Shas is a political party headed by ultra-Orthodox Jews of Middle Eastern origin, purporting to represent Israelis who have been left behind in the distribution of benefits. The subtleties of coping make analysis as risky as their use in governance. Critics may have only a partial grasp about policy-makers' intentions.

Coping that goes bad resembles improvisation that is attempted by an unskilled speaker or musician.[23] The problems may range from minor snafus in programme administration, undisciplined or irresponsible behaviour, to major organizational chaos or policy that is wasteful of resources and productive of more social and economic harm than benefit. While supporters may claim that coping has found and exploited opportunities, opponents may link it to a waste of time and resources. Critics use terms such as 'dilettante' and 'opportunist'. The writings of Yehezkel Dror express both positive and negative assessments of coping. He has praised creative inspiration as an essential trait of policy-makers who must deal with new and challenging conditions.[24] He has also condemned 'hand to mouth' policy-making as a poor way of responding to events without adequate planning.[25] Luck plays its part. Success depends partly on the actions or inaction of others. The situation is similar to that in sports. A player who departs from the expected may be cheered as brilliant. If the same action goes wrong, the player may land on his rear and suffer the boos of the crowd.[26]

The late prime minister of Israel Yitzhak Rabin spoke out against a culture of improvisation, or what he termed, 'rely on me'. He described it as sloppiness and irresponsibility. His own death was due partly to the slovenly way that security personnel handled assignments. Their lack of disciplined attention to the rules allowed a number of unchecked civilians, including Rabin's assassin, to congregate in the area where the prime minister's vehicle was to meet him after a rally.

By the nature of coping and related behaviours, results are not likely to be applauded universally. These ways of dealing with serious problems may lack direction and lead nowhere but from one crisis to another. They may work best in close-knit communities with extensive areas of implicit agreement, such as families and small communities, or when two sides in a dispute are forthcoming, generous, understanding and accommodating. Ambiguity may be most likely to facilitate accommodation when it is not defined precisely, and where contending parties are not compelled to recognize what they have lost.

The problems with ambiguity and other forms of coping are built into the situations that encourage them. By their nature, chronic problems have no obvious solutions. Keeping conflict moderate and avoiding a worsening of a crisis are admirable goals when the alternatives are worse.

It helps to have a sense of direction, but the path through difficult problems is likely to be one of detours. Observers and participants alike may not perceive the outcomes likely to be produced by one manoeuvre or another.

NOTES

1. See my 'The Promised Land of the Chosen People Is Not All That Distinctive: On the Value of Comparison', *Israel Affairs*, Vol. 5, Nos. 2–3 (Winter–Spring 1999), pp.279–92.
2. For more extensive documentation, see my 'Israel: A Metropolitan Nation-State', *Cities*, Vol. 14, No. 6 (1997), pp.363–9.
3. Y. Gradus, 'The Emergence of Regionalism in a Centralized System: The Case of Israel', *Environment and Planning D: Society and Space*, Vol. 2 (1984), pp.87–100.
4. Erik Cohen, *The City in the Zionist Ideology*, Jerusalem: Hebrew University Institute of Urban and Regional Studies, 1970.
5. E. Razin, 'Metropolitan Reform in the Tel Aviv Metropolis: Metropolitan Government or Metropolitan Cooperation?', *Environment and Planning C: Government and Policy*, Vol. 14 (1996), pp.39–54.
6. For more extensive documentation, see my 'The Israeli State: A Cumbersome Giant', *Israel Studies*, Vol. 2, No. 2 (1997), pp.242–59.
7. Data for 1993 shows Israel in first place. *World Data 1995: World Bank Indicators on CD-ROM* (Washington, DC: International Bank for Reconstruction and Development/World Bank, 1995). Data for 1995 shows Israel in a group of leading states, trailing behind The Netherlands, Sweden, Belgium and France. www.worldbank.org.
8. Joseph Heller, *God Knows*, New York: Dell Publishing Company, 1984, p.256.
9. Ira Sharkansky, 'Israeli Civil Service Positions Open to Political Appointments', *International Journal of Public Administration*, Vol. 12, No. 5 (1989), pp.731–49; and *Annual Report for 1996*, Jerusalem: Civil Service Commission, 1996, p.175 (in Hebrew).
10. State Comptroller's Office, *Annual Report No. 47*, Jerusalem: State Comptroller's Office, 1997, pp.838–55 (in Hebrew).
11. Daniel J. Elazar and Chaim Kalchheim (eds.), *Local Government in Israel*, Lanham, MD: University Press of America, 1988; and Frederick A. Lazin, *Policy Implementation and Social Welfare: Israel and the United States*, New Brunswick, NJ: Transaction Books, 1986.
12. Gregg Barak, 'Toward a Criminology of State Criminality', in Gregg Barak (ed.), *Crimes by the Capitalist State: An Introduction to State Criminality*, Albany: State University of New York Press, 1991, pp.3–16; and Daniel E. Georges-Abeyie, 'Piracy, Air Piracy, and Recurrent US and Israeli Civilian Aircraft Interceptions', in Barak, *Crimes by the Capitalist State*, pp.129–44; Avner Yaniv (ed.), *National Security and Democracy in Israel*, Boulder, CO: Lynne Rienner Publishers, 1993; Dan Horowitz and Moshe Lissak, *Trouble in Utopia: The Overburdened Polity of Israel*, Albany: State University of New York Press, 1989; *Israel Law Review*, Vol. 23, Nos. 2–3 (Spring–Summer, 1989); Michael Shalev, *Labour and the Political Economy in Israel*, New York: Oxford University Press, 1992; and Baruch Kimmerling (ed.), *The Israeli State and Society: Boundaries and Frontiers*, Albany, State University of New York Press, 1989.
13. Amos 5: 22–24.
14. A. Friedberg, B. Geist, N. Mizrachi and I. Sharkansky (eds.), *State Audit and Accountability*, Jerusalem: State Comptroller's Office, 1991; State Comptroller's Office, *Report on the Results of Expenditure Audit of Political Groups for the Period of the Election to the 13th Knesset: 1.1.92 to 31.7.92*, Jerusalem: State Comptroller's Office, 1993 (in Hebrew).
15. State Comptroller's Office, *Report on the Results of Expenditure Audit of Political Groups for the Period of the Election to the 13th Knesset: 1.1.92 to 31.7.92*, Jerusalem: State Comptroller's Office, 1993 (in Hebrew).
16. *Jerusalem Post*, 5 Feb. 1993, p.1.
17. This section relies on my *Ambiguity, Coping, and Governance: A View of Politics and*

Policymaking Having General Application Based on Israeli Experiences, Westport, CT: Praeger, 1999.

18. David Biale, *Power and Powerlessness in Jewish History*, New York: Schocken Books, 1987.
19. William E. Connolly, *Politics and Ambiguity*, Madison: University of Wisconsin Press, 1987.
20. *Kal Ha'ir*, 19 June 1998, p.82 (in Hebrew).
21. *Jerusalem Post*, 22 May 1996, p.5.
22. Asher Friedberg and Ira Sharkansky, 'Ambiguities in Policymaking and Administration: A Typology', *International Journal of Organization Theory and Behavior*, Vol.1, No.1 (1998), pp.1–17.
23. See Ira Sharkansky and Yair Zalmanovich, 'Improvisation in Public Administration and Policy Making in Israel', *Public Administration Review*, Vol.60, No.4 (July–August 2000), pp.321–9.
24. Yehezkel Dror, *Public Policymaking Reexamined*, San Francisco: Chandler Publishing Company, 1968.
25. Yehezkel Dror, *Improving Policy and Administration in Israel*, Tel Aviv: Library of Management, 1978 (in Hebrew).
26. Dan E. Inbar, 'Improvisation and Organizational Planning', in Robert V. Carlson and Gary Awkerman, (eds.), *Educational Planning: Concepts, Strategies, and Practices*, New York: Longman, 1991, pp.65–80.

Controlling Government: Budgeting, Evaluation and Auditing in Israel

ROBERT SCHWARTZ

Administrative control has been at the heart of public administration discourse for the greater part of the twentieth century. Perhaps the dominant characteristic of modern public administration is its focus on hierarchic bureaucratic control structures. Financial control is a key component of bureaucratic systems designed first to curb abuse of public funds and later to restrain public spending and to promote efficient and effective use of resources. Efforts to promote efficiency and effectiveness have been supported by various types of evaluative activity including policy analysis, programme evaluation, performance monitoring and value-for-money auditing.

The past decade witnessed attempts in many countries at substantial reform in their approach to administrative and financial control. In the view of some observers, these managerial reforms constitute a paradigm shift from bureaucratic to post-bureaucratic control.[1] Despite substantial differences among reforms enacted by various countries,[2] post-bureaucratic control elements generally include: decentralization to autonomous governmental units and to state or local government; introducing competition by increasing the use of private and voluntary sector providers and opening bidding to a number of government agencies; cutting red-tape procedure-based control mechanisms; focusing on results – outputs, outcomes or a combination of the two.

While managerial reforms promote decentralized autonomy and flexibility, emphasizing competition-based control, a number of commentators note that, at the same time, they actually strengthen central control. For example, Paul Hoggett argues that ostensibly autonomous agencies created in the UK:

> nevertheless operate within a field or arena in which the hand of central government remains strong. It both liberates and enslaves ... The centre retains control over key strategic question such as the

Robert Schwartz is a lecturer in the Department of Political Science at Haifa University.

allocation of resources to operational units and the framework of financial and personnel rules and performance targets within which devolution over operational matters is allowed to occur.'[3]

In a similar vein, Christopher Hood warns against dichotomizing bureaucratic and post-bureaucratic control systems, claiming for example, that 'new public management' reforms include elements of both competition and compliance review.[4]

Evaluation has an important role to play in the post-bureaucratic regime. Performance measurement and programme evaluation are essential tools for assessing the work of decentralized government units, lower levels of government, private and voluntary sector service providers.

A further development in administrative control, in at least one country, is the advent of what has been termed the 'audit society':

> In the United Kingdom the rate of growth of state audit bodies, for example the National Audit Office and the Audit Commission, has been striking since they were established in the early 1980s. At the same time, the rise of auditing in the medical field and the emergence of markets for environmental auditing and quality assurance have been prominent subjects of discussion ... Formal audit and evaluation mechanisms have been installed in universities and schools ... Very few people have been left untouched by these developments; the need to give more and better accounts and to have these accounts checked by auditors has become widespread.[5]

This article presents a snapshot of administrative control in Israel at the end of the twentieth century and reviews developments over the past decade. It examines the extent to which financial control conforms with bureaucratic as opposed to post-bureaucratic premises, assesses the role played by evaluation and explores the extent to which Israel can be considered an audit society.

Budgeting, evaluation and auditing in Israel necessarily reflect the general state of public administration. Accounts in recent years depict public administration in Israel as highly centralized and predominantly hierarchic–bureaucratic.[6] Although the government has formally accepted strong post-bureaucratic premises in recommendations made by a public commission, little has been implemented.[7] In fact, there has been no major reform of Israel's public administration system in its short 50-year history.

BUDGETING

Allocation

Recent portrayals place Israeli budgeting squarely in the hierarchic–bureaucratic realm. The Kubersky Commission on administrative reform assessed the state of budgeting in Israel as of ten years ago. The Commission report notes that the current budget is a line-item budget characterized by great detail, which not only detracts from the ability to get a general overview and to focus on the important, but also hurts managerial flexibility. For when the budget is so detailed, administrators have almost no room for deciding on changes in ways to achieve the objectives. Furthermore, the budget system is orientated to describing inputs, predominantly financial inputs to salaries and projects. The budget does not include information about programmes, outcomes, outputs or achievements of any sort.

The Commission characterizes the budgeting process as incremental: in general it relates only to additions or deletions from the existing base. The need for and justification of existing activities is not assessed in a methodical and systematic fashion. The overall attention paid to these programmes is sporadic and incidental. In practice existing programmes have a sort of immunity in the existing budget system.

Finally, the Commission assessed the relationships between the Budget Division and the various government ministries, noting that the Budget Division does not restrict itself to determining the overall budget framework for ongoing activities and development programmes – or supervision to ensure that ministries don't go beyond this framework; in practice, the Division intervenes in the ongoing management of each ministry and discusses its expenditure items in great detail.[8]

David Dery provides a comparative quantitative measure of the centralized nature of Israeli budgeting. He notes that in 1993 Israel's national budget included 7,314 budget items – as compared to about 700 in each of Denmark, The Netherlands and Sweden.[9]

One expression of the bureaucratic–hierarchic model in financial control is the strict annuality of the budget process. Funds must be spent during the financial year for which they are appropriated. Unspent funds are not made available for spending in the following year. Furthermore, low spending on a particular budget item leaves agencies open to cuts in that item in ensuing years. This type of bureaucratic rigidity has been identified as a significant fetter on the flexibility of public managers.[10]

Spending

Central controls on spending complete the picture of hierarchic–bureaucratic financial control over central government. Heading up the spending control system is a network of deputy accountant generals dispatched to all government bodies. These employees of the Ministry of Finance must authorize all disbursements, contracts and other financial obligations. It is their responsibility to ensure that expenditures are conducted in accordance with the detailed itemized budget and to prevent misuse of funds and overspending. The extent of centralized control of spending is evident from the accountant general's online computer linkages to all individual ministry accounting offices. This system 'is designed to streamline financial management and control in the ministries and provide online, updated, detailed information on financial operations'.[11]

Formally, ministries have no authority to 'overspend' or to transfer funds from one area to another. Transfers between 'major units' require the approval of the Knesset Finance Committee. Transfers between 'minor units' require the approval of the Budget Department in the Ministry of Finance. Since deputy accountant generals must sign each expenditure, they are in an excellent position to ensure that ministry spending follows these rigid guidelines. The Principles of the Budget Law of 1985 stipulates the cessation of activities started, cancellation of contracts signed and dismissal of workers hired where adequate coverage in the budget is lacking, and it makes it a disciplinary offence for civil servants not to abide by the restrictions set in the annual Budget Law.

Interviews with senior officials reveal general agreement that, for the most part, the deputy accountant general system successfully prevents major financial abuses. At the same time, ambiguous definitions and political pressures on deputy accountant generals result in some bending of rules. One official reports, from personal experience, that, 'Deputy accountant generals who make waves are moved out'.

State Comptroller's Office reports provide some evidence of system breakdowns. In one case, the deputy accountant general for the Ministry of Housing and Construction did not prevent overspending commitments of more than $40 million – 20 per cent over the approved budget – to contractors for constructing housing for new immigrants.[12] The same deputy also did not prevent the ministry from diverting allocations for residential construction to non-budgeted activities, including aid to settlements and to voluntary organizations for constructing public buildings, sports fields and tennis courts.

Contrasting with tight executive control on spending, the Knesset has virtually no role in this arena. In other countries such as the UK, a standing legislative committee – the Public Accounts Committee – considers the accounts of each government department along with the financial audit of these accounts conducted by the National Audit Office. Public expenditure is also examined by the Select Committees of the House of Commons, which study in detail the activities of government departments and require the attendance of ministers and officials for cross-examination.[13]

In Israel, the State Comptroller's Office (SCO) conducts a financial audit only of the general national accounts and relates to the accounts of individual government bodies only by the way as part of operational audits. Deputy accountant generals draw up budget implementation reports, on a cash basis, regarding each ministry. These are formally submitted to the Knesset Finance Committee, but receive little attention there or in any other Knesset committee. This contrasts sharply with the accrual-based financial reporting adopted by many countries which is designed to enable a clearer view of the financial viability of government activities.

Israeli budget implementation reports consist of a straight report on amounts spent as compared to amounts approved. SCO reports point out several deficiencies in this type of reporting:

- The reports do not include information about actual commitments made for expenditure in the coming year as compared to allocations for such commitments. As a result the legislature receives no report as to such occurrences as an 878 per cent increase in commitments for future expenditures made by the Ministry of Construction and Housing in 1990 – from $367 million to $3,589 million.
- Comparison is between actual spending and total amounts approved including changes approved over the course of the budget year which can be significantly different from original allocations.
- There is no accounting for changes in capital, meaning that the parliament is provided no knowledge of a significant part of government incomes and expenditures.[14]

Financial Control of the Margins

Centralized bureaucratic financial control also dominates government relations with organizations external to central government, including local authorities, third sector organizations and universities. A common thread in these control relationships is that potentially strong bureaucratic control mechanisms are in place, but their activation is weak.

Government budgeting of local authorities for example is characterized by detailed budget items. A recent SCO report notes that the Ministry of Education funds local authorities through some 255 different budget items allowing no freedom for local authorities to transfer funds.[15] David Dery describes a similar situation in the area of social welfare.[16] Ostensibly, local authorities have little power over the determination of these budget items and no authority to transfer funds among budget items. Kalcheim however, suggests that weak overseeing on what local authorities actually do with the money means that in practice they are much less constrained than appears.[17]

Financial control over third sector organizations that receive grants from government ministries follows a similar pattern.[18] In place are apparently strong central control mechanisms. The Law of Associations requires associations to register with the Ministry of Interior, submit annual audited financial statements, and maintain proper bookkeeping practices. The law also grants the registrar the power to conduct investigations of an association's management and operations, and to recommend to a court that an association in violation be dismantled.

While the Law of Associations appears to provide for extensive accountability of associations,[19] the SCO has found severe shortcomings. Many associations submit financial reports beyond the deadline, or do not submit them at all. The registrar has limited means for analysing the financial reports. And the registrar has conducted few investigations of associations.[20]

A 1997 ministerial directive requires that grants committees of ministries hire accountants to check the financial affairs of grantees and internal auditors to conduct operational audits of the use of grants to achieve objectives. The results of this directive are not yet apparent. One study of the decisions taken by these committees suggests a flaw in their structure. 'The clerks who serve on grants committees report to the minister and rely on him for their advancement. Their ability to protest the favouring of an association depends on their willingness to endanger their standing in the ministry'.[21]

Control of universities provides a final example of strong mechanisms and weak enforcement. The government provides the bulk of funding to universities through the Planning and Budgeting Committee of the Council of Higher Education. The committee is responsible for bureaucratic overview of the execution of university budgets. SCO reports show that this overview did not prevent universities from accumulating tens of millions of dollars in debt in the 1980s.[22] A recent report chastises the committee for neglecting to develop indicators for measuring the efficient management of university resources.[23]

The picture that emerges from this presentation of budget allocations and spending is one of centralized, process-orientated control. In both allocations and spending, we find seemingly strong bureaucratic control mechanisms which display weaknesses in their implementation. There is little evidence of decentralized financial control or of managerial flexibility in return for results-focused control.

Yet tight bureaucratic financial control has been identified as an impediment to efficiency as for example, in the following portrayal of the American case:

> ... federal managers dutifully spend just about every federal dollar provided to them. They have little flexibility and take few risks, and even when they see opportunities to spend money more wisely, they have little discretion to do so ... They see their job as spending the money provided by Congress according to rigid rules that preclude initiative or discretion.[24]

To rectify these problems, America's National Performance Review prescribed a series of financial management changes.[25] Budgeting should be made more flexible by restructuring appropriations controls to reduce over-itemization and aligning them with programmes. At the same time, detailed restrictions and earmarks in appropriations hearings and report language should be reduced. Agencies should be permitted to carry over 50 per cent of their unobligated year-end balance in operating funds into the next fiscal year. And more appropriations should be converted to multiyear or no-year status and the reprogramming of funds should be expedited.

In order to increase managerial autonomy, employment ceilings and floors should be eliminated and managers should be held accountable for operating within budget. The president should develop performance agreements with agency heads, and agencies should devise performance agreements committing themselves to achieve organizational goals and objectives. Finally, planning and measurement efforts should be accelerated in every federal agency and performance objectives and results incorporated as key elements in budget and management reviews.

The need for reform of Israel's financial control apparatus was recognized in 1989 by the Kubersky Commission. Implementation of the following Commission recommendations would have moved Israel a long way in the direction of post-bureaucratic financial control:[26] enhance the managerial capacity of the directors general by granting them greater discretion and flexibility within the framework of results-orientated administration; adopt results-orientated management by creating three-year plans that set performance targets for each ministry and by linking budgets to performance; transfer authority from the Budget Division of the Ministry of Finance to the operating units; use internal and external audits as a managerial tool for assessing results rather than monitoring procedures.

Despite the adoption of the Kubersky Commission report by the government, none of the recommendations connected with financial control has been implemented. Galnoor, Rosenbloom and Yaroni squarely blame the Budget Division:

> The Budget Division of the Ministry of Finance neither recognized management reforms as a worthwhile enterprise for the attention of its owns economists nor allowed other government units to undertake them. Having a de facto monopoly on approving reforms with budgetary consequences (namely, in their belief, any change), the division has effectively blocked any such efforts.[27]

Further evidence of the Budget Division's power comes from the fate of a little known government decision. In July 1993, the government decided to grant freedom of action to government ministries to conduct internal transfers of funds among budget items – subject to compliance with a number of criteria.[28] Not only has this decision not been implemented, but senior officials of the Accountant General's Division and the State Comptroller's Office are not even aware of its existence.

EVALUATION

Evaluation plays a role in both bureaucratic and post-bureaucratic control models. In the bureaucratic model, evaluation was first developed as part of attempts to rationalize budgeting and decision-making regarding social programmes. It was initially conceived mainly as a tool for helping senior officials and politicians in deciding on the most rational (cost-beneficial) courses of action and for holding programme executioners to account. The post-bureaucratic model emphasizes output and outcome performance measurement, used both for assessing the performance of managers and for budgeting. Not connected with either control model, evaluation has also emerged as an important internal management tool.

Evaluation and Programme Budgeting

In programme budgeting – in its various reincarnations including PPBS, ZBB, MBO, PAR and PEMS – budget allocations are informed by evaluation. Allen Schick's model of the development of budgeting systems sees in budgets used for planning (based on evaluation) the most mature budget systems.[29] However, an analysis of budgeting, auditing and evaluation in seven countries found that, in general, there is little systematic integration of evaluative information in budgeting.[30] More recently, new public management reforms are once again attempting to integrate evaluative information into the budget allocation process.[31]

Ostensibly, Israel has a programme budget. Since 1976, budget documents classify expenditures by fields of activities or programmes, rather than by administrative units.[32] A closer look at the budget documents reveals, however, that similar programme activities are not always grouped together, but are listed under administrative unit headings. The SCO observes that the change since 1976 to a programme-based classification was 'to a certain extent a semantic one'.

Of course, merely classifying expenditures by programmes – a programme budgeting system doesn't make. While simply changing the classification of expenditures can focus attention on the real cost of specific programmes, the aspired benefits of programme budgeting require sophisticated analyses of costs and benefits of individual programmes as well as comparisons among programmes and programme areas. The question is to what extent the programme-based classification serves analysis aimed at rationalizing budget allocation decisions.

In this context it is important to note that Israel never officially adopted PPBS, ZBB or MBO type budgeting as part of legislated or declared reform. There are thus no systemic mechanisms for the conduct of analysis-based budgeting. The Kubersky Commission noted that:

> The annual budget in its present form, is not an appropriate framework for yearly planning. Government Ministries are not required to present programmes and objectives even for a one year period. The budget requires them to present mainly a detail of their inputs ... Today, the government budget is more a financial document than a plan of action and a framework for decision making ... The structure of the budget and the information included in it do not promote a rational decision-making process which should be focused on goals and objectives and enable analysis of alternatives – including their long-term consequences.[33]

That is not to say that Israeli budgeting completely lacks analysis and evaluation. Various techniques, such as cost–benefit analysis have been used for quite some time.[34] Danieli reports that, for particular programmes, there is continued effort to develop pre-implementation analysis techniques as for example regarding transportation projects, public housing and hospital privatization.

However, according to the Kubersky Commission:

> The need and justification for existing activities are not examined in a systematic and orderly fashion. Comprehensive attention to these programs is sporadic and by chance only. In effect, existing programmes have a sort of 'immunity' under the current budgeting system ... Generally, the need and worthwhile of programs is not examined, there is not analysis of alternatives for implementing projects or objectives, and there are no analyses of efficiency and of effectiveness.[35]

Senior Ministry of Finance officials offer two explanations for the limited amount of evaluative input into the budgeting process: (1) for a large proportion of programmes it is impossible to conduct meaningful evaluation, that is, a basic lack of belief in the ability of social sciences to provide valid evidence; (2) there is no use evaluating existing programmes because ministries are never willing to end them. The senior official in the Ministry of Finance responsible for budgeting methods explains that, from his experience, the politics of the budgetary process in Israel prevents the elimination of existing programmes. Budget proposals by government agencies include requests for funding new programmes, but not at the expense of cutting existing ones. There is no reason to request performance evaluation if political considerations ultimately prevent cutting low performance programmes.

Evaluation for Accountability and Management

In efforts to improve programme accountability, many countries have adopted top–down institutionalization of evaluation practice, requiring government agencies to evaluate their programmes on a regular basis in a systematic fashion.[36] Israel has no directives requiring government agencies to evaluate their programmes on a regular basis. This is not surprising considering the background of bureaucratic–hierarchic control in Israel's public administration environment. Although the Kubersky Commission recommended establishing evaluation units in government ministries, here too the government has not acted.

Despite the absence of a national policy, evaluation practice is alive and well in Israel. To date, evaluation is conducted predominantly at the programme director level. One study of evaluation practice found that Knesset committees did not request government agencies to conduct evaluation studies, did not commission any such studies themselves and used existing evaluation studies only rarely in their supervisory work.[37] Furthermore, it found that ministers and senior bureaucrats only rarely initiated evaluation activity. The study concludes that institutionalized evaluation occurs in only a handful of government agencies. Yet, the incidence of evaluation is relatively high in many other agencies. For the most part, evaluation has been a bottom-up activity, initiated by programme directors who care and, in some areas, by an external not-for-profit research institute. Although evaluation practice is quite widespread, its development can be described as fragmented.

Evaluation restricted mainly to the programme director level has limited potential to serve as a tool of either bureaucratic or post-bureaucratic control because it is not generally used by central executive agencies or by Knesset committees. At most, it might be expected to help line managers improve programme delivery. Schwartz found that a high proportion of the evaluations he reviewed did not deal with questions of outcome effectiveness, thus limiting their potential contribution to post-bureaucratic control.[38]

An exception to this mode of evaluation is the work of the JDC–Brookdale Institute:

> An independent, non-profit organization, the Brookdale Institute operates as a partnership between the American Jewish Joint Distribution Committee and the Government of Israel. Its governing Board includes the Directors-General of the National Insurance Institute and the Ministry of Health and the Deputy Director of the Budget Division in the Ministry of Finance.
>
> Brookdale conducts a wide range of research and policy analysis activities including a lot of evaluation work. Brookdale initiates, persuades and cajoles government agencies to engage in joint ventures

to evaluate services. The evaluation of most of these programs would not take place if program directors were left to their own initiative – largely because of lack of resources.

The Brookdale model constitutes a unique institutionalization of evaluation. The Institute is funded by the interest on an endowment fund created by a private foundation and the Government of Israel, by the American Jewish Joint Distribution Committee and directly by the Government of Israel for specific projects. Ongoing dialogue between Brookdale researchers and government agency staff enables exchange of information regarding evaluation needs. This, along with annual planning meetings with senior agency administrators and their partnership in Brookdale's governing body, facilitates the development of a responsive evaluation program.[39]

Signs of Change

A number of localized developments are making for the institutionalization of evaluation in more agencies and for more widespread practice of evaluation in others. These developments include: legislatively mandated evaluation requirements; expansion of the Brookdale Institute; an increase in the number of frameworks for training evaluators and the recent establishment of the Israeli Evaluation Organization.

National Health Insurance Law: Israel's new National Health Insurance Law, passed in 1994, marks the first time that a major piece of social legislation mandates the conduct of evaluation efforts. The law established a National Health Insurance Council responsible, among other things, for overseeing the implementation of the law by way of evaluation research. A considerable annual budget of some NIS7 million (US$2 million) has been allocated. A comprehensive request for proposals is issued each year for research into various components of the new health care system. To date, the council has funded over 100 studies, many of which are evaluations. It is early to say whether future legislation will follow the National Health Insurance Law in building evaluation into new programmes.

Expansion of the Brookdale Institute: Brookdale's contribution to the development of evaluation practice in Israel was mostly limited until the 1990s to the field of ageing. The institutionalization of evaluation practice in the field of ageing has spurred demand from government agencies for the entrance of Brookdale to other fields. In response, Brookdale established a health policy division in 1989. Subsequently, in the 1990s Brookdale entered the fields of immigrant absorption and disability. In 1995, Brookdale launched a new centre for the study of services for children and youth.

The availability of Brookdale's support provides an opportunity for many programme directors eager to conduct evaluation who were frustrated by resource constraints. The Brookdale model makes it likely that evaluation will become an important tool for programme development and policy-making in the new fields.

Evaluation Training: Israel's major universities now offer courses in evaluation as part of special MA programmes in public policy and public administration. Evaluation courses are also taught in schools of education, schools of social work and public health programmes. In addition, a total of approximately 150 evaluation professionals have participated in an annual week-long evaluation workshop given by Israeli and American evaluation experts.

It remains to be seen whether these changes will lead to greater use of evaluation as a tool of control by central executive agencies and/or by Knesset committees.

AUDITING

According to Michael Power's description, auditing of different sorts is now so pervasive in the United Kingdom's administrative culture as to create an impression that there is always somebody looking over one's shoulder. At first glance, this might seem to contradict the post-bureaucratic premises of administrative reform in the UK. Auditing which, in its traditional form, focuses on verifying compliance with administrative and financial procedural norms is clearly part of the bureaucratic model. Yet in the eyes of some observers, the devolution and decentralization aspects of post-bureaucratic reforms creates increased need for auditing.

> The 'hollowing out of the state' by the NPM generates a demand for audit and other forms of evaluation and inspection to fill the hole ... This is a deliberate erosion of central capability in favour of long distant mechanics of auditing and accounting. Auditing has the qualities of 'portability and diffusion' and apparent 'political neutrality' (Hood, 1991: 8) which serve the programmatic elements of the NPM. The disaggregation and devolution of public service provision require the specific technologies of reaggregation and recentralization which accounting and auditing promise.[40]

Still, auditing of procedural compliance runs counter to the basic premises of the post-bureaucratic model. However, over the past 30 years or so the mandates of Supreme Audit Institutions (SAIs) have been broadened to include economy, efficiency and effectiveness auditing. To the extent that it focuses on the evaluation of results or on the verification of results-orientated reporting, auditing would certainly fit in with the post-bureaucratic approach to administrative control.

The following section reviews the extent to which Israel is developing into an 'audit society' and explores the extent to which it operates in bureaucratic as opposed to post-bureaucratic mode.

The State Comptroller's Office

Over the years, foreign experts, such as E.L. Normanton and Gerald Caiden have noted that Israel's State Comptroller's Office is considered a leader in its field.[41] Israeli political scientist, Asher Arian observes that the SCO is apparently the only national institution working to improve programme performance.[42] A recent report by an independent Israeli research institute, however, is quite critical of the SCO's work.[43]

The scope of SCO audit includes an ever widening range of agencies – providing one indication that Israel is moving towards becoming an 'audit society'. Upon its establishment in 1949, the SCO's remit included government ministries and statutory authorities. In the 1950s the SCO was given responsibility for auditing local authorities and government corporations. In the 1960s and 1970s the audit of political party and election financing was added to the mandate. And in the 1990s, the SCO was authorized to audit the Labour Federation, Histadrut – an umbrella organization which employs some 25 per cent of the labour force.

The State Comptroller Law authorizes investigation of government activities from just about any angle – including bureaucratic model audits of administrative and financial procedures and post-bureaucratic audits which include a look at managerial and outcome effectiveness. The law states explicitly that the State Comptroller's Office is to investigate incomes and expenditures, the management of moneys, legality, economy, efficiency and moral integrity. Furthermore, the law empowers the state comptroller to investigate any other matter which he feels necessary. The law does not explicitly state that the State Comptroller's Office can conduct effectiveness audits. However, the SCO interprets the law as to include effectiveness auditing as well.[44]

The state comproller faces a very large task – fiscal, managerial and programme audit of all government ministries, national authorities, government enterprises and local authorities with an overall budget of more than $54 billion. He is expected to accomplish this with a total budget of some $31 million and a staff of 310 auditors trained in economics, business administration, political science, public administration and law.[45]

The paucity of audit resources relative to the task at hand means that SAIs are faced with tough decisions in choosing among potential audit jobs regarding both which government activities to audit and what type of audit to conduct (bureaucratic or post-bureaucratic orientated). Previous work by Ira Sharkansky[46] suggests that the allocation of scarce audit resources is affected by political considerations of SAIs which seek to attract attention to their reports. He notes that, in choosing audit topics, state audit institutions are invariably influenced by the desire to be relevant and to attract press and public attention. As one of the political actors, state auditors vie with other actors for the limelight. In listing the possible consequences of the expanded role of state audit in Canada, Sharon Sutherland notes, along similar lines, that because their power comes from the media, SAIs will tend to produce reports that are 'meaningful' in lay terms – meaning audits of recognizable, purposeful programmes.[47]

On the other hand, auditors claim that they do not wish to get involved in policy audit, that is, audit of the merits of policy objectives.[48] At least three countries – Australia, Canada and Germany – have prevented their SAIs from conducting effectiveness audits in order to keep them out of policy questions given to partisan political controversy.[49] Other auditors, such as Britain's National Audit Office, are mandated to audit effectiveness, but take great care not to appear to be criticizing the merits of policy objectives.[50]

The auditor thus faces opposing pressures. The need to be relevant and responsive to demands for programme accountability requires the auditor to conduct post-bureaucratic model audits which assess the outcome results of government programmes. One analysis goes so far as to suggest that state auditors be required to conduct effectiveness evaluations 'no matter how politically sensitive the issues might be'.[51] At the same time, the desire to steer clear of partisan political controversy dictates distancing from effectiveness auditing – or at least exercising great caution in its conduct.[52] Another perspective suggests state auditors should focus on revealing corruption and fraud in order to satisfy 'blood-thirsty' media and legislative users.[53]

To what extent is SCO activity commensurate with the post-bureaucratic model? Ira Sharkansky notes a number of instances in which Israel's state comptroller has been quite aggressive in reporting on programme failures linked with misdirected policy decisions.[54] Well-known examples include reports on important issues on the public agenda concerning: the cost-effectiveness of the Lavi jetfighter, the effectiveness of gas masks provided to civilians and the expected impacts of building a major highway (Road no. 6).

Analysis of the SCO's annual report, however, shows that such policy effectiveness audits are exceptions to the rule of rather placid reports on mundane programmes and issues. Analysis of SCO reports reveals that only a small part of the work considers programme effects.[55] In the analysis, all audit reports, conducted over an 11-year period, concerning programmes of the Ministry of Social Welfare, Labour, Health and the National Insurance Institute were classified as traditional audits or programme audits. A total of 84 audit reports were published during the study period concerning 31 of the study programmes. A total of only 12 out of the 84 reports (14.3 per cent) included outcome findings. The vast majority of findings in the audit reports concerned administrative deficiencies. This finding is further supported by an analysis of all audit report findings in the SCO's Annual Report No. 44 (1994). Only 16 per cent of the findings in this report concerned effectiveness or efficiency.

These data indicate that the SCO is primarily orientated to the bureaucratic model. In this the SCO is not significantly different from most other state auditors whose post-bureaucratic audits take second place to their bureaucratic auditing duties.[56] Critical of this tendency, Ira Sharkansky suggests that the scrutiny of procedures is best left to clerks and to internal auditors. He asks, 'Why should auditors be content with checking procedures, when they can use their expertise to assess the effectiveness and efficiency of government activity?'.[57]

While the SCO conducts a limited amount of effectiveness evaluation, it actively encourages auditees to evaluate themselves. In a rare initiative in 1990, the state comptroller issued a letter to government ministers emphasizing the benefits of programme evaluation and encouraging them to develop evaluation capacity in their agencies. The SCO's reports also frequently note that the auditee ought to conduct a study of the effectiveness of the programme under consideration.

State Audit and Administrative Control

There is no lack of mechanisms to connect the SCO with central executive and legislative agencies in order to feed audit findings into systems of administrative and financial control. Existing mechanisms include: the Inspectorate-General's Division in the Prime Minister's Office – responsible for monitoring the correction of deficiencies; the Ministerial Committee for Coordination and Administration which discusses selected audit reports and hands down requests for correction of deficiencies; and the Knesset Committee for Audit Affairs, a standing committee which holds hearings concerning a large proportion of audit reports.

The SCO undoubtedly provides a good deal of material which contributes to both executive and legislative control of the bureaucracy. The scope of its remit suggests that state auditing pervades public activity. However, the SCO can cover only a small part of government activity. And neither executive nor legislative bodies can dictate audit topics. The SCO's contribution to administrative and financial control is therefore quite sporadic and haphazard. Further evidence of its limitations is in the SCO's focus on bureaucratic mode auditing.

Internal Audit

Internal audit is essentially a management function designed to provide organizations with assurances against corruption and waste and to promote efficient and effective programme implementation. To the extent that its findings are restricted to organization management, the contribution of internal audit to administrative and financial control is limited. However, internal audit might indirectly contribute to such control by providing coverage of bureaucratic compliance, thus freeing external state auditors to focus their work on post-bureaucratic performance auditing or on monitoring the functioning of internal control systems.[58]

Passage of the Internal Audit Law in 1992 marked the institutionalization and expansion of internal auditing in Israel and constituted a significant step in the direction of making Israel an 'audit society'. The law requires that internal auditors be appointed in all public bodies, including government ministries, statutory authorities, government corporations and local authorities. It also requires that publicly traded commercial enterprises, banks and insurance companies appoint internal auditors. These stipulations require internal auditing in thousands of organizations. Although no empirical evidence is available, some observers have suggested that because of ambiguities in the law and weak enforcement procedures, internal audit in many organizations is far less advanced than would be expected.

The Internal Audit Law does not establish any division of labour between state auditors and internal auditors; their mandates are very similar. In fact, much of the language in the Internal Audit Law is borrowed from the State Audit Law. Unlike the State Audit Law, the Internal Audit Law explicitly authorizes internal auditors to examine effectiveness. Mizrahi notes that the main difference between state auditors and internal auditors is that internal auditors' reports remain internal and directed towards organizational management whereas state audit reports are published for public consumption and serve as a tool of public accountability. In the absence of any division of labour, state auditors and internal auditors coordinate their work so as to avoid duplication.[59]

There is little evidence as to the extent to which internal auditors actually conduct post-bureaucratic mode audits. Friedberg points out that issues of access complicate research into internal auditing.[60] The best material available comes from SCO reports on internal auditing, but the most recent of these is from 1986 – prior to the enactment of the Internal Audit Law. Among the main findings of this report were that most of the internal audits related to administrative matters, personnel management and ministerial directives; they did not deal with the essence of programme activities.[61]

Anecdotal evidence from internal audit professionals suggests that even after enactment of the Internal Audit Law, internal auditors conduct little results-orientated effectiveness auditing of the post-bureaucratic mode.

Mizrahi writes, for example, that, 'In many cases the state audit focuses on matters that concern the public, whereas the internal auditor is more interested in the administrative aspects. In this sense, the internal audit which concentrates on current administrative matters, complements the state audit dealing with wider public aspects.'[62]

Contrary to what Sharkansky and others might hope, the focus of Israeli internal audit on compliance has not resulted in the SCO focusing mostly on performance. Perhaps explanations offered by Paul Light concerning the work of inspectors-general (IGs) in the United States can help to explain this. Like Israel's internal auditors, American IGs were given a broad mandate to examine both traditional procedural compliance and post-bureaucratic performance and effectiveness. Light shows that IGs have preferred to focus their work on questions of compliance. He attributes this mainly to organizational politics interests of IGs:

> Congress, the president, and the media appear to have much greater interest in the products of compliance monitoring than performance or capacity monitoring ... Those who want headlines in the war on fraud, waste, and abuse will find plenty in the narrow stories of graft and corruption that often flow from compliance monitoring. The media appear always willing to report another story on the subject.[63]

Findings concerning media coverage of state auditing in Israel indicate that similar incentives may lie behind the SCO's focus on compliance auditing. Friedberg shows that the media pay more attention to compliance audit reports than to performance audit reports.[64]

This section has shown that the mechanisms for the conduct of state audit and internal audit provide for the possibility of a significant contribution to extensive internal and external administrative control. Yet scarce audit resources and inadequate enforcement of the Internal Audit Law limit the coverage of both state and internal audit. And auditing remains primarily focused on bureaucratic procedural compliance rather than on post-bureaucratic evaluations of the achievement of results. Even so, the expansion of state and internal audit suggest that Israel is moving in the direction of becoming what Michael Power has called an 'audit society'.

Several additional developments lend further support to the emergence of an 'audit society': multiplicity of auditing of local authorities: internal auditors, Ministry of Interior appointed accountants, Ministry of Interior operational auditors, and state audit; structured measures-based inspection systems for nursing homes; environmental impact reporting to local authorities and in corporate financial reporting.

DISCUSSION

Is Israel's government out of control? The picture which emerges from this review is a mixed one. We find a plethora of financial control and auditing mechanisms. Yet these mechanisms display at least four deficiencies: weak activation, including lack of resources and enforcement; little parliamentary supervision; strong tendencies to focus on bureaucratic procedural compliance at the expense of post-bureaucratic evaluation of results; and poor or non-existent linkages among budgeting, evaluation and auditing. Overall, the picture is not so much one of a government out of control, but rather that of control systems whose effectiveness is questionable. Explanations of the sorry state of administrative control in Israel include agenda overload; highly politicized coalition-type government; and a cultural tendency to lack of thoroughness.

Yehezkel Dror claims that agenda overload causes accountability to be a non-issue in Israel: 'Overload of the public agenda in Israel with critical policy issues, (i.e., defense and foreign affairs) combined with the low estimation of the role of public administration in policy-making, reduces interest in "accountability" of the civil service.' Dror further notes that: 'Lack of authority by the Knesset and its committees to interrogate officials and the legal duty of officials appearing before the legislature and its committees to express only the position of their ministries further strengthen the Knesset's lack of interest in accountability of officials.' Finally, Dror suggests that the closed nature of government in Israel and the general acceptance of the need for secrecy in order to maintain security further hinders supervisory activities.[65]

Governance by coalition combined with a relatively high degree of politicization creates an environment less than conducive to the establishment of effective administrative control. Ira Sharkansky notes that, 'Where politicians control so much of who gets what and how, the appeal of efficient or responsive government may be less attractive ...'.[66] Political appointments, especially at senior levels, are still common in Israeli government agencies, as indicated by the SCO in two recent annual reports.[67] While other forms of blatant political patronage may be decreasing, a former civil service commissioner notes that politics still permeates Israeli administration in more subtle ways.[68]

Ira Sharkansky discusses a cultural characteristic of Israeli administration relevant to our discussion. He points out a number of cases where Israeli administrators failed to follow up on the implementation of programmes. Sharkansky attributes the lack of follow-up to simple indifference.[69] The former prime minister, Yitzhak Rabin, made it one of his missions to fight against this type of non-thoroughness which he called the 'trust me' or 'it will be all right' culture.

What is to be done? While this is not the place for prescription, a couple of caveats are in order. Post-bureaucratic control premises and the audit society motif are used in this article for purposes of comparison, not as norms to aspire to. The word is not yet in on the performance of so-called post-bureaucratic control systems. Indeed there is a body of literature casting doubt on the potential of relying on performance results measurement. Problems include difficulties in constructing proper measures; obtaining data; reliability; interpreting trends and incorporating the information in budgeting and policy-making processes.[70] Much of this is reminiscent of obstacles faced by programme budgeting reforms in the 1960s and 1970s. Israel's conservatism in adopting administrative reforms, for whatever reasons, may serve her well.

Auditing systems, as developed in recent years, provide significant opportunities for effective administrative control. Fuller realization of their potential would see some attempt at division of responsibilities and an orientation of more audit work to the assessment of programme efficiency and effectiveness. At the same time, carrying the audit society to an extreme risks the advent of systems that crumble, 'because of the weight of their information demands, the senseless allocation of scarce resources to surveillance activities and the sheer human exhaustion of existing under such conditions, both for those who check and those who are checked'.[71]

NOTES

1. Michael Barzelay, *Breaking Through Bureaucracy*, Berkeley, CA: University of California Press, 1992; Guy Peters and Donald Savoie, 'Civil Service Reform', *Public Administration Review*, Vol. 54 (1994), pp.418–25.
2. Laurence E. Lynn, Jr., 'The New Public Management as an International Phenomenon: A Skeptical View', *Advances in International Comparative Management*, Supplement 3 (1998), pp.105–22.
3. Paul Hoggett, 'New Modes of Control in the Public Service', *Public Administration*, Vol. 74 (1996), pp.9–32.
4. Christopher Hood, 'Control over Bureaucracy: Cultural Theory and Institutional Variety', *Journal of Public Policy*, Vol. 15 (1996), pp.227–9.
5. Michael Power, *The Audit Society: Rituals of Verification*, Oxford: Oxford University Press, 1997, p.3.
6. Yitzhak Galnoor, David Rosenbloom and Allon Yaroni, 'Creating New Public Management Reforms: Lessons from Israel', *Administration and Society*, Vol. 30 (1998), pp.393–420; David Dery and Emanuel Sharon, *Economics and Politics in Budgetary Reform*, Jerusalem: Israel Democracy Institute, 1994 (in Hebrew); Haim Kubersky, *Report of the Committee for Review of the Civil Service and Government Funded Bodies*, Jerusalem: Government Printer, 1989 (in Hebrew).
7. Galnoor *et al.*, 'Creating New Public Management Reforms'.
8. Kubersky, *Report of the Committee for Review*, pp.84–95.
9. David Dery, *Introduction to Public Administration Unit Six*, Tel Aviv: Open University of Israel, 1997, p.182 (in Hebrew).
10. Al Gore, *From Red Tape to Results: Creating a Government that Works Better and Costs Less*,

Washington, DC: Government Printing Office, 1993, p.195.
11. State Comptroller's Office, *Audit of Government Financial Statements and Reports*, Jerusalem: State Comptroller's Office, 1994, p.6.
12. State Comptroller's Office, *Annual Report No. 42*, Jerusalem: State Comptroller's Office, 1992, p.169.
13. John J. Glynn, *Public Sector Financial Control and Accounting*, 2nd edn, Oxford: Blackwell Publishers, 1993, p.131.
14. State Comptroller's Office, *Annual Report No. 42*, p.170.
15. State Comptroller's Office, *Annual Report No. 48*, Jerusalem: State Comptroller's Office, 1998, p.312.
16. David Dery, *Who Governs Local Government*, Jerusalem: Israel Democracy Institute, 1994, p.79 (in Hebrew).
17. Haim Kalcheim, *Local Government in the Weave of the Democratic State*, Jerusalem: The Jerusalem Institute for Public Affairs, 1997 (in Hebrew).
18. Robert Schwartz and Ira Sharkanksy, 'Collaboration with the "Third Sector" – Issues of Accountability: Mapping Israeli Versions of this Problematic', paper presented at the Public Administration Committee Annual Conference, Collaborative Government: Concepts, Experience and Outcomes, Sunningdale, England, 6–8 Sept. 1999.
19. Yael Yishai, 'State and Welfare Groups: Competition or Cooperation? Some Observations on the Israeli Scene', *Nonprofit and Voluntary Sector Quarterly*, Vol. 19 (1990), pp.215–36.
20. State Comptroller's Office, *Annual Report No. 47*, Jerusalem: State Comptroller's Office, 1997, pp.590–603.
21. Amnon DeHartog, 'State Support of Public Institutions – the Blooming of Special Monies', *Mishpatim* Vol. 29 (1998), pp.75–107.
22. State Comptroller's Office, *Annual Report No. 37*, Jerusalem: State Comptroller's Office, 1987; Ira Sharkansky, 'Israel's Political Economy', in Ehud Sprinzak and Larry Diamond (eds), *Israeli Democracy Under Stress*, Boulder, CO: Lynne Rienner, 1993, p.160.
23. State Comptroller's Office, *Audit of Institutions of Higher Education*, Jerusalem: State Comptroller's Office 1999, p.24.
24. Al Gore, *From Red Tape*, p.185.
25. Summarized in Allen Schick, *The Federal Budget: Politics, Policy, Process*, Washington, DC: The Brookings Institution, 1995, p.186.
26. Summarized by Galnoor *et al.*, 'Creating New Public Management Reforms', pp.402–3.
27. Ibid., p.412.
28. Shimon Danieli, 'Government Budgeting', in Aharon Kfir and Jakob Reuveni (eds.), *Public Administration in Israel Towards the 2000s*, Tel Aviv: Tcherikover Publishers, 1998, p.184 (in Hebrew).
29. Allen Schick, 'Macro-Budgetary Adaptations to Fiscal Stress in Industrialized Countries', *Public Administration Review* (March/April 1986), pp.124–34. [???]
30. Andrew Gray and Bill Jenkins, 'Horses to the Water: Budgeting, Auditing, and Evaluation in Seven Governments', in Andrew Gray, Bill Jenkins and Bob Segsworth (eds.), *Budgeting, Auditing & Evaluation: Functions & Integration in Seven Governments*, New Brunswick: Transaction, 1993, pp.186–95.
31. June Pallot, 'Newer than New Public Management: Financial Management and Collective Strategy in New Zealand', *Advances in International Comparative Management*, Supplement 3 (1998), pp.125–44; James Guthrie, Olov Olson and Christopher Humphrey, 'Lessons from Public Sector Financial Management Change in OECD Nations', *Advances in International Comparative Management*, Supplement 3 (1998), pp.255–72.
32. State Comptroller's Office, *Audit of Government Financial Statements and Reports*, 1994, p.14.
33. Kubersky, *Report of the Committee for Review*, p.79.
34. M. Sandberg and H. Stoessel, 'Budget Preparation and Management in Israel', *International Review of Administrative Sciences*, Vol. 31 (1965); David Weinshal, 'Planning and Budgeting in Israel – Problems and Experience', *Public Finance*, Vol. 27 (1972); Shimon Danieli, 'Government Budgeting', p.183.
35. Kubersky, *Report of the Committee for Review*, p.85.
36. Auditor General of Canada, *Program Evaluation*, Report of the Auditor General of Canada to the House of Commons, Ottawa: Auditor General of Canada, 1993; Australian National Audit Office, *Implementation of Program Evaluation – Stage 1*, Audit Report No. 23,

Canberra: Australian National Audit Office, 1990.
37. Robert Schwartz, 'The Politics of Evaluation Reconsidered: A Comparative Study of Israeli Programs', *Evaluation*, Vol. 4, No. 3 (1998), pp.294–309.
38. Ibid., p.307.
39. Jack Habib, 'Making the Link between Policy and Research in the Field of Aging: Some Lessons from Israel', in *Approaches to Linking Policy and Research in Aging: Israel and Florida Report of a Conference*, Jerusalem: JDC–Brookdale Institute of Gerontology and Adult Human Development, 1991, pp.35–60.
40. Power, *The Audit Society*, p.44; Christopher Hood, 'A Public Management for All Seasons?', *Public Administration*, Vol. 69 (1991), p.8.
41. E. Leslie Normanton, 'Reform in the Field of Public Accountability and Audit: A Progress Report, in Benjamin Geist (ed.), *State Audit: Developments in Public Accountability*, London: Macmillan, 1981, pp.55–80; Gerald E. Caiden, 'New Directions in State Audit', in Geist, *State Audit*, pp.151–4.
42. Asher Arian, *Politics in Israel: The Second Generation*, Chatham: Chatham House, 1985.
43. Gad Barzelay and David Nachmias, *The State Audit Institution: Authority and Responsibility*, Jerusalem: Israel Democracy Institute, 1998 (in Hebrew).
44. Miriam Ben-Porat, 'The State Comptroller and Supreme Court Decisions', *Iyunim Bi'bikoret Ha'medinah*, Vol. 53 (1995), pp.7–25.
45. Robert Schwartz, 'State Audit – Panacea for the Crisis of Accountability? An Empirical Study of the Israeli Case', *International Journal of Public Administration*, Vol. 23, No. 4 (2000), pp.405–34.
46. Ira Sharkansky, 'The Politics of Auditing Reconsidered', *Iyunim Bi'bikoret Ha'medinah*, Vol. 38 (1984), pp.35–9.
47. Sharon L. Sutherland, 'The Politics of Audit: The Federal Office of the Auditor General in Comparative Perspective', *Canadian Public Administration*, Vol. 29 (Spring 1986), pp.118–48.
48. Ira Sharkansky, 'Israel's Auditor as Policy-Maker', *Public Administration*, Vol. 66 (Spring 1988), pp.77–90.
49. Robert Schwartz, 'Coping with the Effectiveness Dilemma: Strategies Adopted by State Auditors', *International Review of Administrative Sciences*, Vol. 65, No. 4 (1999), pp.511–26.
50. David A. Dewar, 'The Auditor General and the Examination of Policy', in Asher Friedberg, Benjamin Geist, Nissim Mizrahi and Ira Sharkansky (eds.), *State Audit and Accountability: A Book of Readings*, Jerusalem: State Comptroller's Office, 1991, pp.95–102.
51. Jane Broadbent and Richard Laughlin, 'Evaluating the "New Public Management" Reforms in the UK: A Constitutional Possibility', *Public Administration*, Vol. 75 (1997), p.501.
52. Michael Barzelay, 'Central Audit Institutions and Performance Auditing: A Comparative Study of Organizational Strategies in the OECD', *Governance: An International Journal of Policy and Administration*, Vol. 10 (1997), pp.253–60; Andrew Gray, Bill Jenkins and John Glynn, 'Auditing the Three Es: The Challenge of Effectiveness', *Public Policy and Administration*, Vol. 7 (1992), pp.56–69.
53. Paul Light, *Monitoring Government: Inspectors General and the Search for Accountability*, Washington, DC: The Brookings Institute, 1993, p.19.
54. Sharkansky, 'Israel's Auditor as Policy-Maker'.
55. Schwartz, 'State Audit – Panacea for the Crisis of Accountability?'.
56. Robert Schwartz, 'State Audit in Developed Democracies', in Friedberg, *et al.*, *State Audit and Accountability*, pp.240–254.
57. Sharkansky, 'The Politics of Auditing Reconsidered', p.37.
58. Sharkansky, 'The Politics of Auditing Reconsidered'; Power, *The Audit Society*, p.133.
59. Nissim Mizrahi, 'State Audit and Internal Audit in Israel', in Asher Friedberg, Benjamin Geist, Nissim Mizrahi and Ira Sharkansky (eds.), *Studies in State Audit*, Jerusalem: State Comptroller's Office, 1995, pp.205–20.
60. Asher Friedberg, 'Professional Audit in Israel: Introduction and Background', in Friedberg *et al.*, *Studies in State Audit*, 1995, p.15.
61. State Comptroller's Office, *Annual Report No. 36*, Jerusalem: State Comptroller's Office, 1986, pp.886–93.
62. Mizrahi, 'State Audit and Internal Audit in Israel', p.216.
63. Light, *Monitoring Government*, p.19.

64. Asher Friedberg, 'State Audit, Politics and the Media', in Friedberg *et al.*, *State Audit and Accountability*, pp.110–131.
65. Yehezkel Dror, 'Public Administration in Isael', in Donald C. Rowat (ed.), *Public Administration in Developed Democracies: A Comparative Study*, New York: Marcel Dekker, 1988, pp.357–75.
66. Sharkansky, 'Israel's Political Economy', p.168.
67. State Comptroller's Office, *Annual Report No. 39*, Jerusalem: State Comptroller's Office, 1989, pp.627–44 and *Annual Report No. 41*, Jerusalem: State Comptroller's Office, 1991, pp.595–618.
68. Galnoor *et al.*, 'Creating New Public Management Reforms', p.399.
69. Ira Sharkansky, *What Makes Israel Tick*, Chicago: Nelson-Hall, 1985, p.140.
70. Neil Carter, Rudolf Klein and Patricia Day, *How Organisations Measure Success: The Use of Performance Indicators in the Public Sector*, London: Routledge, 1992, pp.125–51; Arie Halachmi and Geert Bouckaert (eds.), *Organizational Performance and Measurement in the Public Sector*, Westport, CT: Quorum, 1996; Peter Smith, 'On the Unintended Consequences of Publishing Performance Data in the Public Sector', *International Journal of Public Administration*, Vol. 18 (1995), pp.277–310; General Accounting Office, *Managing for Results: Analytic Challenges in Measuring Performance*, GAO/HEHS/GGD-97-138.
71. Power, *The Audit Society*, p.2.

Judicial Accountability in Israel: The High Court of Justice and the Phenomenon of Judicial Hyperactivism

YOAV DOTAN

INTRODUCTION

Widespread consensus exists that law, courts and politics are important for three sets of activities that are central to every modern state: policy-making, social control and regime legitimation. The role of courts in society and the relationship between the judiciary and the other branches of government vary in different states and cultures. While no widely accepted paradigms exist which model the relationship between law, courts and politics in a cross-national context, it is widely acknowledged that the role of judicial institutions is becoming ever more central to processes of policy-making both in the context of various national states and in the international arena. The phenomenon known as judicial activism was once viewed as a uniquely American practice. It is now, however, clear that judicial activism is rising in many countries across the globe.[1]

This article has a dual purpose: first, I intend to describe the general characteristics of the judicial system in Israel and its relationship with other social institutions in the Israeli society. Second, I will describe a model of society within which the courts (and, in particular, the Supreme Court) play a paramount social role by routinely intervening in the practices of the public administration as well as in the business of other governmental and non-governmental institutions, and thereby bringing about a judicialization of society. By the term 'judicialization' I mean not only that the courts intervene – on an almost routine basis – in decision-making processes of other institutions, but also that this widespread intervention brings about a process of adaptation to patterns of legal

Yoav Dotan is a senior lecturer at the Faculty of Law, Hebrew University, Jerusalem.

thinking and judicial decision-making by many other administrative institutions. I will call this model of highly intensive judicial intervention 'judicial hyperactivism'.

JUDICIAL REVIEW IN ISRAEL: AN OVERVIEW

Historical Background

Israel has no complete, formal constitution. When Israel was established in 1948 after 30 years of British Mandate, the question of forming a constitution was self-evident. The promise of a constitution was even mentioned in the Declaration of the Establishment of the State of Israel (1948) – the first official document of the state. Accordingly, the declaration vested in the first elected Knesset the power to form a constitution for the state. Owing to the strong disagreement between different political forces and against the background of national security crisis following the 1948 war, the first Knesset declined to form any constitution. Instead, it was decided, in 1950, that the constitution would be enacted gradually, chapter by chapter in the form of 'Basic Laws' in the future. While the Knesset did use its power to enact Basic Laws during the first 45 years of independence, most of these dealt with the institutional aspects of Israel's constitutional system, and did not include entrenched clauses. Therefore, the power of the courts to review ordinary legislation on the ground of unconstitutionality was not regarded as a valid constitutional principle, and the English concept of parliamentary supremacy presided over jurisprudential thinking for more than four decades.[2] In 1992 two Basic Laws dealing with the protection of fundamental human rights were enacted. Thereafter, the question of the power of the courts to strike down legislation that contradicts the Basic Laws became increasingly dominant within the constitutional discourse. On 1995 the Supreme Court ruled that the new Basic Laws of 1992 brought about a 'constitutional revolution' after which the Court has power to strike down ordinary legislation whenever it contradicts the provision of any Basic Law.[3] Despite the rhetoric of the Court, nowadays Israel has yet neither a complete written constitution nor a full bill of rights. Important constitutional principles such as the separation of powers are not included in any constitutional text, and fundamental political rights, such as freedom of speech and freedom of religion, are not entrenched in any Basic Law.[4]

The absence of a written constitution did not preclude the Israeli courts from developing judicial review over administrative actions. Since the formation of the state the courts, led by the Supreme Court, developed a wide array of principles and doctrines in order to review the actions of the bureaucracy, the military and other administrative institutions. Shortly after Israel was established, and in the middle of a war that seriously threatened the very existence of the state, the Supreme Court struck down a decision made by military authorities to detain an Arab resident of Jaffa, using their powers under emergency regulations. The Court ruled that the detention was illegal owing to the failure of the authorities to follow the procedure set by the regulations, and ordered the release of the detainee. It added the following words: 'The authorities are bound by the law like any other citizen in the state. And the rule of law is one of the fundamental principles of the state.'[5] This statement of the principle of rule of law was followed by a number of cases in which the courts developed principles and doctrines to serve as tools for judicial review, such as the principle that government agencies should not exceed the powers bestowed on them by the legislator, and the requirement that agencies should follow not only the written letter of the law but also its underlying purposes, and refrain from abuse of discretion. Other principles developed by the courts were the principle of equality and the prohibition against discrimination, as well as procedural requirements of fairness in administrative actions.[6]

At the same time the courts used creative techniques of statutory interpretation in order to establish legal principles for the protection of individual rights. A good example is the celebrated decision in the *Kol Ha'am* case. There, the Supreme Court struck down a decision of the Minister of the Interior to order the suspension of the publication of a communist newspaper for a period of ten days. The ministerial order was issued after the newspaper published some articles that criticized the state's foreign policy and were regarded by the government as containing false information that was harmful to the public interest. The Court ruled that the government is not allowed to use its powers to restrict the freedom of the press unless it can demonstrate that the restriction is necessary owing to an immediate and serious danger for the security of the state or the public order. There was nothing in the language of the Press Ordinance, on which the minister founded his initial action, that pointed to the creation of such a requirement. The Court, however, used the Declaration of Independence as a canon of interpretation, in order to read into a British-colonial ordinance – which was enacted in order to restrict the freedom of the press – some constitutional principles taken from the jurisprudence of constitutional democracies with an established bill of rights.[7] Using similar interpretative techniques the Supreme Court developed protection for other human rights such as freedom of demonstration and procession, freedom of association, freedom of occupation and the right for privacy.[8] The willingness of the Court over the years rigorously to develop such human rights' protection by using creative methods of statutory interpretation and by resorting to foreign jurisprudence of established constitutional democracies (such as the US and Canada) has granted those principles a semi-constitutional status. In principle, these judicially acknowledged freedoms were always subject to infringement by clear-cut language of the Knesset. In practice, however, the Knesset seldom used its sovereign supremacy in order to limit those freedoms and seldom used legislative initiative in order to reverse such judicial reforms. These developments led some commentators to view these rulings as Israel's 'unwritten constitution' that contain, among other principles, 'an unwritten bill of rights'.[9]

The Structure of the Judicial System

The judicial system of Israel is divided into two main types: one, the general law courts, known as the civil or regular courts; and the other, tribunals and other authorities with judicial powers. The difference between the two types is, *inter alia,* in their jurisdiction: while the jurisdiction of the law courts is regarded as general, the jurisdiction of the tribunals is limited in terms of persons or matters or in both aspects and in accordance with the directives of the legislation that created the relevant tribunal.

The Israeli legal system recognizes various types of tribunals, the most important of which are the military courts, the labour courts and the religious courts, the latter enjoying exclusive jurisdiction in matters such as matrimonial status and dissolution of marriage. In addition, there are various other administrative tribunals created by law in order to deal with appeals from administrative agencies determining social benefits, tax liability, compensation for injury, allocation of agriculture quotas, etc. More recently the Knesset established tribunals having a much broader sets of quasi-judicial functions, such as the Standard Contracts Tribunals and the Restrictive Trade Practices Tribunal that plays an increasingly important role in regulating uncompetitive practices. A general principle controlling the activity of all tribunals is that their decisions are always subject to review by the general courts. The review process is conducted either by an appeal to a regular civil court (most frequently the District Court) in accordance with a specific order in the relevant statute that deals with appeal procedures, or, in the absence of such specific order, by the Supreme Court, sitting as the High Court of Justice (see below).[10]

The regular court system has three levels: the Supreme Court, District Courts and Magistrates' Courts. The two latter levels are trial courts dealing with both criminal and civil matters, and they are distinguished according to the gravity of the matter. The District Courts also hear appeals on decisions of the Magistrates' Courts. The Supreme Court in Israel serves in three different capacities: as a court of *cassation,* as a court of appeal and as a court of first (and last) instance for judicial review cases. The Court serves as appellate court for cases tried initially by the District Courts. It also serves as a third instance of *cassation* for a handful of cases that have been tried by the Magistrates' Courts, appealed to the District

Courts and then appealed again to the Supreme Court after receiving a special permission.[11]

The third function of the Supreme Court, and the most important for the purposes of the current discussion, is its function to hear petitions in administrative matters while sitting as the High Court of Justice (HCJ). In this capacity the Supreme Court functions in essence as *a trial court* for a substantial portion of all administrative cases reaching litigation. This means that the Supreme Court sitting as HCJ has the primary jurisdiction for judicial review cases in Israel, and functions as both first and last judicial instance for all the cases it hears in this capacity. The jurisdiction of the HCJ to hear judicial review cases as first and last instance exists under the orders of the Basic Law: The Judiciary, in any administrative case, unless a statute specifically designates another court to fulfil this function. Over the years the HCJ itself developed rules under which some administrative cases such as in the field of public tenders and zoning and planing are directed to the lower courts for judicial review.[12] In any of these cases, whether the case was referred to the lower court under the order of a statute or according to the precedents set by the HCJ itself, the Court always retains the discretionary power to review the case either in the trial stage or as an appellate court. The practical meaning of this structure is that there is no decision within the Israeli government, judicial tribunals or any other public agency, that is not potentially subject to review by the HCJ. The Court holds full discretion on whether to review any governmental decision, and there are no formal jurisdictional constraints precluding it from reviewing any decision, should it decide to do so. It also means that many judicial review cases will make their way directly to the Supreme Court regardless of the question of the value of the claim or the legal importance of the matters involved. This judicial structure, which is quite unique to Israel, combined with some other characteristics of the HCJ that will be discussed below, has profound implications on the process of judicial review and on its place in Israeli society.[13]

The last element of the judicial system that needs to be discussed here is the office of the attorney general. The attorney general (AG) in Israel, similar to her counterpart in Britain, is the chief legal adviser to the government and the head of the prosecution. In her capacity as legal adviser to the government the AG is the head of the government legal service which includes both a large apparatus of advisers within the Ministry of Justice and all legal advisers in all government ministries. The AG's office enjoys exclusivity in this function of giving legal advice to all parts of the government, and its opinions and directives are binding – according the ruling of the Supreme Court – for any governmental authority. In her second capacity, the AG is the head of the national litigation branch, which includes, in addition to the criminal department, other departments in various fields of law. The AG possesses the exclusive power to represent the state, or any state agency, in all courts, tribunals and in all matters.[14] This wide array of powers makes the attorney general a key position in the Israeli government as well as in the legal system as a whole. The importance and the prestige related to this position is also emphasized by the fact that many of the lawyers who have served as attorney generals were appointed to the Supreme Court after completing their tenure.

Most important for the purpose of this article, the AG holds the exclusive power to represent the state or any other governmental authority before the HCJ. The representation is normally performed by a small department within the office of the AG. This department, usually composed of no more than a dozen lawyers, is responsible for the representation of all government authorities (excepting only local municipalities) before the HCJ. These lawyers handle the representation on behalf of the respondents in over 80 per cent of all cases litigated before the HCJ, and appear before the justices of the Supreme Court on an almost daily basis. Therefore, its members acquire special expertise in HCJ litigation and enjoy a high reputation within government circles as well as with the justices of the Supreme Court itself.[15]

Judicial Independence

The Israeli judiciary enjoys a high level of independence and autonomy *vis-à-vis* the other branches of the government. Judicial independence is a principle protected by the Basic Law: The Judiciary. Independence is also fortified by the fact that the judges of the civil courts of all levels are appointed for a permanent tenure that continues until retirement at the age of 70. Judges enjoy salaries that are very high in comparison to other public employees. They cannot be removed from office except by a decision of the Court of Discipline, consisting of judges appointed by the president of the Supreme Court, or upon a decision of the Judge's Election Committee at the proposal of the minister of justice or the president of the Supreme Court. The canon of judicial autonomy in Israel is, however, the system of appointment of judges. The appointments of judges at all levels are made the by Judges' Election Committee. The Committee is composed of nine members. It includes the president of the Supreme Court and two other Supreme Court judges, the minister of justice and one other minister (traditionally a jurist by training), two members of the Knesset (of whom one is traditionally a member of the opposition) and two representatives of the Israeli Bar. This composition ensures that the process of appointment is almost entirely immune from any pressures or influences on the part of the government, political parties or any other organization outside the judiciary itself, since the majority in the Election Committee are not party politicians. Furthermore, a convention exists that a candidate for the Supreme Court will not be selected if the choice is not acceptable to the representative of the Court. This convention is but one aspect of the dominance of the Supreme Court in the process of selecting judges. The whole process is bureaucratic and almost entirely hidden from the public eye or media coverage. The names of the potential candidates remain secret till a very late stage, and the content of the Election Committee's discussions remains covert.[16] The three representatives of the Supreme Court appear in the committee after coordinating their positions with all other members of the Supreme Court, and therefore are able to speak with unanimity in the committee. All these factors result in a situation in which the selection of judges is heavily influenced by the justices themselves with very little influence from the political branches or any other external forces. Last but not least, the high level of public support and relative popularity of the judiciary within the Israeli public buttresses the independence of the judiciary. This latter factor ensures that while the government is capable, in principle, of infringing on the independence of the judiciary by resorting to legislative reforms in the Knesset, it would be slow to take such initiatives. Indeed, attempts made by the government to infringe on the autonomy of the court system, rare as they have been, brought about strong public opposition and were unsuccessful. Thus, for example, when in 1998 the government sought to appoint to the position of attorney general a loyal party supporter devoid of serious professional credentials, the decision brought about an almost unprecedented wave of public criticism that forced the government to change the candidate.[17]

THE JUDICIAL ACTIVISM OF THE HCJ

The 'Old Court' – from Establishment to 1980

Although the HCJ was always considered an influential institution within the Israeli polity it is possible to distinguish between different stages regarding its overall impact on society. From the establishment of the state and until the late 1970s the Supreme Court, while gradually and consistently developing a rich jurisprudence of judicial review, kept a fairly low public profile. As described earlier, the Court established firmly the principles of the rule of law, and enjoyed almost absolute obedience to its rulings on the part of the bureaucracy even where such rulings were opposed to government policies. It also developed principles and tools of judicial review and protections of basic human rights, as mentioned above. All this was done, however, without much direct judicial involvement in political controversies and current public debates.

The fact that the Court managed to keep its distance from such political involvement was not fortuitous. A number of doctrines and strategies were adopted by the Court to ensure minimal exposure to intensive political involvement. First, the Court imposed strict limitations on the ability of litigants to raise political issues in court. The concept of *standing* adopted by the HCJ during this period was designed to keep the Court within the safe boundaries of an institution whose main function is to decide controversies between individuals and the state rather than issues reflecting clashes of interests between opposing sectors in society. In order to meet the requirement of standing, the petitioner had to show direct and substantial interest in the state action at stake. The Court held that a mere infringement upon religious feelings or ideological convictions of the petitioner is unlikely to satisfy this requirement.[18] Moreover, even when the petitioner could show that the state action caused her some *material* damage, she was likely to be denied standing if the same action caused similar harm to a large group of other people or to the whole sector of which she formed a part. This narrow concept allowed the Court to refrain from interfering in sensitive political issues in the areas of religion and state, and law enforcement with respect to high-ranking political figures.[19] One important implication of this policy was that it reduced significantly the ability of political parties, interest groups and other organized litigators to use the Court as an arena to promote their political agenda.

The rules of standing were not the only factor inhibiting the use of litigation by organized interests. Another concept with similar effects was *justiciability*. During this period the Supreme Court adopted a narrow concept of justiciability. Under this concept the Court decided that petitions involving issues of foreign policy, military actions or other questions concerning sensitive political issues were considered 'unsuitable' for judicial determination and therefore non-justiciable.[20] The Court also adhered to a narrow concept of judicial review. In particular, the HCJ reflected unwillingness to take a close look at certain areas of state activities of major importance. Thus, even when the Court was willing to deal with some matters of sensitive political implication, it developed doctrines that substantially narrowed the scope of review in those matters. For example, the Court adopted a narrow concept of review regarding decisions taken by the military and other security agencies.[21] It also adhered to a remarkably narrow concept of review regarding prosecutorial decisions, stating that only in extreme cases of clear *mala fides* it would be willing to interfere with the decisions taken by the Attorney General or other prosecutorial authorities.[22] Apart from these legal principles there were a number of other informal strategies and tactics that were aimed to keep the Court away from political controversies and to preserve its low public profile. Thus, for example, the opinions given by the justices were relatively short and their reasoning was often founded on professional, legal and technical-procedural arguments rather than on broad policy statements and value-judgements.[23] The justices tried to reach consensus while sitting on the bench. Political conflicts among the justices were often framed and presented as professional disagreements between legal experts rather than frictions caused by opposing moral or political convictions. The low political profile of the Court was also preserved since the justices refrained almost entirely from expressing their views on legal matters as well as on other issues while not on the bench, and from appearances on the media.[24]

The 'New Court' – Judicial Activism since 1980

The 1980s saw a major shift in almost all the aspects of judicial review mentioned above. There was a dramatic change in the principles concerning access to the courts. In its landmark decision in *Ressler v. Minister of Defence,* the Supreme Court reversed its prior rulings on the issues of standing and justiciability. On the issue of justiciability, Justice Aharon Barak (currently chief justice) said:

> Any [human] action is susceptible to determination by a legal norm, and there is no action regarding which there is no legal norm determining it. There is no 'legal vacuum', in which actions are taken without the law having anything to say about them. The law encompasses any action ... The fact that an issue is 'strictly political' does not change the fact that such an issue is also 'a legal issue'.[25]

Similar revisions were made on the issue of standing. In the early 1980s, the Court was already willing to acknowledge the standing of a petitioner who was substantially harmed by a certain state action even if she belonged to a larger group of people which suffered similar harm. The Court went on specifically to acknowledge the standing of individuals representing interests of a larger sector, such as in the case of consumer protection and environmental issues. The Court also acknowledged at that stage that the ideological nature of the interest of the petitioner should not serve as grounds to deny standing.[26] It was not, however, until the decision in the *Ressler* case that the new concept of standing was presented, completely revising the older case law. In the *Ressler* case, the Court decided that whenever a petition raises an issue of important constitutional merit, or when there is a suspicion of serious governmental violations of the principle of the rule of law, *any* person is entitled to bring the petition into court, *regardless* of her personal interest in the outcome of the litigation. This decision marked a major shift in the position of the Supreme Court as to its self-image concerning its role in society. The Court overtly acknowledged its duty to serve as the guardian of the rule of law, rather than merely as a forum designated for the adjudication of conflicts between the individual concerned and the state.[27]

The reform of the rules concerning the access to court was followed by a similar revision of the rules of judicial review. During the 1980s and the

1990s, the Court showed a growing tendency to expand the scope of judicial review. It developed new tools for judicial review and imposed new requirements on administrative authorities such as the duties of reasonableness, rationality of the decision-making process and proportionality.[28] The Court also revealed willingness to review actions of institutions which were previously held partly or wholly immune from judicial supervision, such as the military and the security services.[29] The HCJ also revised its deferential attitude towards prosecutorial institutions. It ruled that prosecutorial discretion is susceptible to judicial review as is any other administrative discretion. This ruling paved the way for a number of successful attacks on decisions of prosecutorial authorities not to prosecute prominent members of the political, military and financial elites.[30] Moreover, the Court became increasingly involved in government decisions concerning nominations of senior public officials in all sectors. It struck down nominations of senior government officials and high military officers. The grounds for intervention were either that the nomination was motivated by party calculations rather than by professional considerations, or that the nominee was involved at some point in the past in a public scandal and therefore the nomination was unreasonable.[31] In 1993 the HCJ ordered Prime Minister Yizthak Rabin to dismiss a minister and a deputy minister from his government after they were indicted for allegedly committing criminal offences.[32] Last, but not least, in 1981 the HCJ decided that it has jurisdiction to hear petitions dealing with the internal procedures of the Knesset. This decision opened the gate for a long series of petitions in which the Court was asked to intervene in various kinds of decisions and activities taken by the Knesset, its committees and other parliamentary organs.[33]

The reforms of the legal doctrines were accompanied by a wide range of changes in the style of judging. The decisions of the Supreme Court became much longer and more elaborate. The justices base their reasoning on broad principles of law, moral judgements and social policies. Terms such as 'reasonableness', 'the values of the legal system' and so on became increasingly common within the Court's rulings. Unlike their counterparts in the previous era, the judges of the Court today deal explicitly and at length with general issues of law and policy even if they are not directly related to the specific question raised by the case at stake. Some judges (most notably the chief justice, Aharon Barak) are intensively involved in academic writing, and they often meet in camera with members of Knesset as well as with other public figures.

One direct implication of the above-described changes was the rise of organized litigants in the HCJ. The willingness of the Court to review almost any public action and any official decision without limitations such as standing and justiciability enabled interest groups as well as politicians and political parties to resort to the Court on almost any public issue. The

HCJ became a tempting forum for organized interests to carry out their political agenda through litigation. Apart from its activist policies there are several other characteristics of the HCJ that make the Court a favourable forum from organized interests' point of view. The access to the Court is extremely easy. Court fees are minimal and amount to the equivalent of $100. The risk of incurring heavy expenses in case of defeat is also minimal.[34] On the other hand, the benefits that an interest group or a political figure can obtain through litigation are significant. The Court enjoys a high reputation and prestige among the Israeli public. Its rulings are carefully obeyed by the Israeli bureaucracy even when they include mere comments and recommendation without any official or positive orders. Moreover, litigation before the HCJ is intensively covered by the media. Therefore, interest groups may derive symbolic benefits as well as public exposure even when they do not win at the litigation itself. As a result, studies show a sharp increase in the volume of organized interest litigation before the HCJ since 1980. For the same reasons there is a similar rise in the volume of petitions issued by political parties, Knesset members and candidates in elections to the HCJ.[35]

THE MODEL OF JUDICIAL HYPERACTIVISM

In the previous sections I described how during the last two decades the HCJ became a key player within the Israeli polity. There is hardly a political controversy, an issue of public importance or a contemporary moral dilemma that does not find its way, sooner rather than later, as the subject of a petition to this judicial forum. The above description, however, does not fully address the questions of the *mechanisms* by which the Court exerts its enormous influence on society and the overall social implication of its activities. In order to illustrate these issues I shall use the following example.

On 9 May 1999, a week before the general elections, the minister for internal security issued, under his powers according to the Emergency Defence Regulations (1945) an order of closure of some institutions and offices of the Palestinian Authority (PA) in Jerusalem, including, most notably, the Palestinian headquarters at the Orient House in East Jerusalem. The Orient House has been for some years the diplomatic centre of the PA and had been recognized by several foreign governments as a symbol of support for Palestinian political claims regarding the status of the city. It was also visited by many foreign diplomats and heads of states. Therefore, it was expected that the order, had it been carried out by the Israeli police, would have caused an international crisis. It was also feasible that the enforcement of the orders would have stirred a wide range of violent clashes between Palestinian activists and Israeli security forces. No less clear was the fact that the timing of the issuance of those orders was not fortuitous. The orders were issued by the minister after heavy pressures exerted on him by the prime minister at that time, Benjamin Netanyahu, who was facing a defeat in the forthcoming elections and sought to create a political crisis on the issue of Jerusalem.

Less than 48 hours after their issuance, the closure orders were challenged in a petition to the HCJ. If one imagines a 'normal' world of relations between the judiciary and the executive (for example, the one that existed in Israel in the pre-activist era until the late 1970s), it would be easy to present a wide range of practical reasons, judicial doctrines and procedural techniques that would prevent the Court from any intervention in such a matter. For it is hard to imagine a hotter potato on the Court's docket. The combination of the international implications with the immediate political implications on the upcoming elections, should have – on the face of the matter – led the Court summarily to dismiss the petition without getting to the merits. The ground for such dismissal could have been either that the government action involved 'an Act of State', or the lack of justiciability. Moreover, the petition was not issued by any person with a direct interest in the issue at stake. Neither the PA nor any of its organs were listed among the petitioners. Instead, the petition was issued by a group of Israeli left-wing activists, who had no formal connection whatsoever to the institutions against which the orders were directed. Therefore, any court in this hypothetically 'normal' world would have summarily dismissed the petition for lack of standing. Furthermore, on the face the matter it was hard to see on what grounds the petition was based on the merits. According to the relevant emergency regulations the minister had wide discretion to issue the closure orders, provided only that some procedural requirements were fulfilled. Since the relevant procedures were indeed followed, it was highly unlikely that the Court would have any basis to intervene in the discretion of the minister on the merits.

Nevertheless, the HCJ did not summarily dismiss the petition. Instead, the single judge before whom the petition was brought for preliminary hearing immediately issued an intermediary writ ordering the respondents to refrain from enforcement of the closure until further hearing takes place. She also ordered the respondents to issue a statement regarding their position within seven days. The seven-day period was to end a day *after* the elections, but the respondents made no attempt to appear in Court at an earlier stage in order to ask for the revocation of the intermediary order. Instead they stayed their response for a while, and some weeks later the petition was removed with consent of all parties. Therefore, the crisis created by the issuance of the closure order was prevented through the mechanism of the Court's intervention.[36]

This episode, in which no final judgment of the HCJ was given, no opinion was written, and no discussion on the merits took place illustrates some of the more subtle, but no less important aspects of judicial activism. First, it should be noted that the Court is able to have an enormous impact on the bureaucracy and the political system without the need to issue a formal judgment, and without the need for an *actual valid legal cause* that would be needed in order to found such judgment on the merits.[37] Second, there is the crucial issue of the *timing* of review. It should be noted that the HCJ is probably the only Supreme Court in the world that can influence any state action *while it is taking place and in real time.* Unlike most of its counterparts (such as the Supreme Court of the US, the House of Lords in England, etc.), since the Court serves as a first (and last) instance for judicial review, it preserves full discretion to intervene immediately in *any* public issue that is brought before it.

Moreover, over the years the HCJ has developed doctrines and techniques that are meant to ensure that it will have the formal power as well as the practical capability to interfere immediately in any public controversy. The Court established its authority to review not only government organs and public authorities but also other supervisory bodies such as the attorney general (see above), the military prosecutor, all legal advisers in the various ministries, the state comptroller and ombudsman, as well as investigation committees of all kind. It created a pyramid of legal supervision over which the Court itself presides and is capable of intervening in any matter at any stage should it wish to do so. It also used a creative interpretation to free itself from any formal constrains as to its legal jurisdiction and vigorously developed an array of judicial remedies that enable it to confront different needs.

More generally it can be argued that the HCJ has managed to a large extent to break the traditional limits of the adjudicative process. Courts normally suffer from three types of constraint preventing them from acting as effective political players. First, courts are passive institutions. They have no direct control over their own agenda, but rather they depend on external players (namely litigants) to place the issue on the court's docket. Moreover, courts have no control over the timing of the judicial treatment of a given matter. A case may be brought to litigation too early or too late for effective judicial treatment without the ability of the Court to control the timing.[38]

The HCJ has overcome this constraint of passivity by developing and encouraging the activity of interest groups that specialize in litigation. I described above the development of the legal doctrines and procedural conditions enabling interest groups to petition the HCJ. As a result of these developments there are dozens of such organizations, each specializing in a different area (such as human rights, minority rights, environmental issues, judicial watch against misbehaviour of public employees, etc.). These organizations function as 'professional carriers of petitions to the HCJ'.[39] For many of them, issuing petitions is the principal course of action if not the exclusive one. Owing to their activity, there is hardly any possibility that in any given political scandal or public controversy there will not be someone who will bring the Court into the picture.

Another paramount quality of courts that contributes to their incapacity as policy-makers is formality. Adjudication is a remarkably formal process in comparison to other processes of policy-making. It is based on legal reasoning. It is confined to the set of rules and principles embodied in statutes, regulations and previous judicial decisions. The formality of adjudication is also reflected in the heavy restrictions on the channels of communication between the decision-maker and other players. In an adversarial system, a court of law is confined to the arguments raised by the parties. Courts are normally not allowed to advance arguments and policies on their own initiative that were not presented by the parties. Heavy formal constraints also restrict the ability of such courts to gain access to information. The only information that is allowed is that which comprises admissible evidence. The courts are not allowed to initiate factual investigation, to use existing information not admissible as evidence or such as was not presented by the parties. In most cases, a court has also very limited avenues to communicate even with the parties to the litigation, let alone with other players who form no part of the formal process. The process of communication is public and formalized. It is done only in the courtroom, in the presence of both parties, and under rigid procedural requirements. Informal channels of communication, which are so vital to the ability of political institutions and policy-makers to foster their agenda, are almost completely out of the courts' disposal.

Here, again, the HCJ differs remarkably from other judicial institutions. The process of adjudication in the HCJ is extremely informal. Normally, the adjudicative procedure is composed of hundreds of detailed rules and regulations. Not so in the HCJ. There is a handful of basic procedural rules outlined in simple language.[40] The parties are required to support their statements by affidavits. Oral testimonies and cross-examinations are normally not allowed. The attitude of the justices towards the procedural requirements is also extremely informal. On many occasions the arguments of the petitioners are based on information taken from the press or on official or semi-official reports not admissible in regular courts of law. This conception of informality and flexibility reflects also the legal philosophy of the judges and the way they interpret the law (see below).

A third set of confines has to do with the piecemeal and focal nature of adjudication. In its origin, adjudication is a process designed for one main purpose: providing a decisive and authoritative solution to a conflict between two opposing parties by applying an existing set of clear rules (the law) to a concrete set of facts. The judicial procedure is well equipped for this. It is ill equipped to deal with broad questions of policy. Policy-making by courts is piecemeal and incremental. Very often a change of judicial policy relates to a limited point of law, and leaves broad areas of obscurity as to the general impact of the decision on the relevant field of social activity. Unlike other kinds of incremental decision-making, adjudication does not enjoy the quality of reversibility. Courts have no means systematically to collect data, to evaluate the broad effects of a given decision (such as the price of the implementation of a certain court order), to assess priorities and so forth. Courts also lack the ability to monitor over time the process that follows certain decisions and thus the ability to evaluate its correctness.[41]

The HCJ has developed an original strategy by which it aims to overcome some of these limitations. It employs the legal apparatus of the state as an ancillary mechanism operating under its direct, albeit informal, supervision. It often orders the government lawyers appearing before the Court to conduct factual investigations and report to the Court on their findings. It also conducts a follow-up survey on the outcomes of its own decisions. The Court does this by the following technique: in complicated public matters, where the Court believes that the government should issue a comprehensive reform, it sometimes decides to suspend the litigation and allow the government some time to develop the new policy. The government lawyers are ordered to supervise the implementation of the reform by the relevant public authority, while the Court orders both parties to appear before it at some future date (which can be after several months) and report on the outcome of the process. The Court is able to utilize the government lawyers for these purposes owing to the concentrated structure of the government representation before the HCJ. As described earlier, the government is always represented before the HCJ by a small group of lawyers belonging to a special department in the Ministry of Justice. This has contributed to the creation of a special relationship of trust between the judges and this group of lawyers, who function, in essence, as 'officers of the Court' no less than as representatives of their clients.[42]

CONCLUSION: HYPERACTIVISM AND THE JUDICIALIZATION OF THE ISRAELI SOCIETY

So far I have dealt with the phenomenon of judicial hyperactivism from the point of view of the judicial system itself. Judicial hyperactivism, however, has a profound impact on the activities of many other social sectors including the bureaucracy, the political branch that will be discussed only briefly.[43] The creation of a powerful and hierarchical mechanism of judicial review, which is able to interfere in any administrative action in real time, has brought about a process of an almost complete judicialization of the Israeli bureaucracy. The picture of senior government officials, army generals and their like marching to their offices accompanied by lawyers has become commonplace in the Israeli media. The question of whether a certain decision is capable of sustaining judicial review has become an essential part of any bureaucratic decision-making process. The degree of involvement of legal aspects and judicial consideration is such that it is even an essential part of the military when planning all sorts of active operations.[44]

Even more remarkable are the implications of judicial hyperactivism on the political system. Obviously, the willingness of the Supreme Court to second-guess political choices of all kinds created strong incentives for politicians (particularly opposition members) to challenge public policy through litigation after attempts to change it through the political process have failed. Likewise, the possibility of judicial review of legislation has an impact on the ways in which both the Knesset and the government create legislation of all kinds. The intensity of the judicial involvement, however, carries much wider strategic implications. In order to demonstrate this let me return to the Orient House case discussed in the previous section. As explained, the Court intervened in the closure decision only so far as to issue an intermediary order that could have been subject to revocation at any stage. Why was it, then, that Netanyahu's government refrained from issuing an immediate motion to revoke the judicial writ (a motion that had all the chances to be successful)? The most probable answer is that the government was not at all interested in such move. All the prime minister was looking for was a way to demonstrate his commitment to the issue of Jerusalem before the elections. This was achieved by the very fact that the orders were issued. The interference by the HCJ was well anticipated by the decision-makers. It enabled the government to enjoy the political benefits entailed from the very issuance of the orders, without bearing the consequences of enforcing them. In other words, the government, in fact, sought the judicial intervention that allowed it to shift the blame on to the Court for preventing an action that it was not interested in carrying out in the first place. The Orient House case demonstrates how deeply judicial review has become involved in bureaucratic and political decision-making in Israel, and how such involvement may be utilized and manipulated not only by the reviewing courts but also by those institutions that are the subject of review.

NOTES

1. Herbert Jacob, Joseph Sanders and Erhard Blankenburg, *Courts, Law and Politics in Comparative Perspective*, New Haven, MI: Yale University Press, 1996; C. Neal Tate and Torbjorn Vallinder (eds.), *The Global Expansion of Judicial Power*, New York: New York University Press, 1995. There is no widespread consensus as to what the term 'judicial activism' constitutes, and there are different dimensions for activism. Among other factors, activism may be described by the degree to which the court is willing to negate policies adopted through majoritarian processes; the degree to which it is willing to alter earlier court decisions; the degree to which it makes substantive policy choices and the degree of specificity of such policy statements; see B.C. Canon, 'Defining the Dimensions of Judicial Activism', *Judicature*, Vol. 66 (1983), p.236. It is also clear that different courts may be considered 'activist' regarding some of these dimensions, and 'non-activist' regarding other dimensions.

2. D. Barak-Erez, 'From an Unwritten Constitution to a Written Constitution: The Israeli Challenge in American Perspective', *Columbia Human Rights Law Review*, Vol. 26 (1995), p.309. The only exception is the Basic Law: The Knesset (1958) that included an entrenched clause which required a special majority by the Knesset for any legislation directed to change the principle of general, proportional and equal elections. In 1969, the Supreme Court struck down an elections statute that contradicted the entrenched clause while not standing the requirement of special majority during legislation (H.C. 98/69 *Bergman v. Minister of Finance* 27 (2) P.D. 785). While the Court did overrule the Knesset in this case, it used a rather narrow constitutional approach and rejected any future attempts to broaden this precedent into a full concept of constitutional review. See C. Klein, 'A New Era in Israel's Constitutional Law', *Israel Law Review*, Vol. 6 (1971), p.368; H.C. 148/73 *Kaniel v. Minister of Justice* 27(1) P.D. 794.

3. C.A. 6821/93 *Bank Hamizrachi Hmeuchad v. Migdal* 49(4) P.D. 221. Despite its proclamation as to the power of the judiciary to strike down legislation, the Supreme Court refrained in that case from so doing on the merits of the specific statue at stake. Recently, however, the Court did strike down some clauses in a statute on the ground that they were found to be in contrast to the requirements of the Basic Law: Freedom of Occupation (H.C. 1715/97 *Lishkat Menahlei Hashkaot v. Minister of Finance* 51(4) P.D. 367).

4. The two Basic Laws of 1992 are: Basic Law: Freedom of Occupation and Basic Law: Human Dignity and Liberty. The latter law includes some basic rights such as the freedom of movement, privacy and the protection of property, but does not include any clause relating to freedom of speech, freedom of procession or freedom of association.

5. H.C. 7/48 *El-Karbotli v. Minister of Defence* 2 P.D. 5, 15.

6. H.C. 98, 105/54 *Lezarovitz v. The Food Inspector* 10 P.D. 40; Itzhak Zamir, 'Administrative Law', in Itzhak Zamir and Allen Zysblat (eds.), *Public Law in Israel*, Oxford: Oxford University Press, 1996, p.18.

7. H.C. 73, 87/53 *Kol Ha'am v. Minister of the Interior* 7 P.D. 871; B. Bracha, 'The Protection of Human Rights, *Israel Yearbook of Human Rights*, Vol. 12 (1982), p.110; Allen Zysblat, 'Protecting Fundamental Human Rights in Israel without a Written Constitution', in Zamir and Zysblat, *Public Law in Israel*, p.47.

8. H.C. 148/79 *Saar v. Minister of the Interior and the Police* 34(2) P.D. 169; H.C. 241/60 *Kardosh v. The Company Register* 15 P.D. 1151; H.C. 1/49 *Begerano v. Minister of Police* 2 P.D. 80; H.C. 370/79 *Katalan v. The Prison Service* 34(3) P.D. 294.

9. Barak-Erez, 'From an Unwritten Constitution to a Written Constitution'; Zysblat, 'Protecting Fundamental Human Rights in Israel'. It should be noted, however, that the protections given by this unwritten bill of rights were severely limited in some respects. They could not withstand direct legislation aimed at infringing human rights. They were also able to ameliorate only to some extent the impact of emergency legislation (mostly British legislation that was preserved by Israel after the establishment of the state). And they were applied by the courts in a much less activist manner in favour of Arab-Israelis and Palestinians in the context of state security than towards the Jewish population in other contexts. R. Shamir, '"Landmark Cases" and the Reproduction of Legitimacy: The Case of Israel's High Court of Justice', *Law and Society Review*, Vol. 24 (1990), p.781; Y. Dotan, 'Judicial Rhetoric, Government Lawyers and Human Rights: The Case of the High Court of Justice During the Intifada', *Law and Society Review*, Vol. 33, No. 2 (1999), p.319.

10. Zysblat, 'Protecting Fundamental Human Rights in Israel'.
11. The fact that the Court serves a triple function has wide implications on its caseload. The Israeli Supreme Court is an extremely busy judicial institution. The 14 judges, sitting normally in panels of three, have to cope with thousands of cases brought before them each year. For example, in 1993, the Court dealt with over 1,400 appellate cases, a similar number of *cassation* cases and over 1,000 other lawsuits, apart from the 1,171 HCJ petitions which were disposed by it during that year. The number of cases increases constantly each year (see *Yearbook of the Central Bureau for Statistics of Israel* 1993). The question of how 14 judges (sitting normally in panels of three) can manage to cope with such a huge caseload and still function both as the Supreme Court and the principal tribunal for judicial review is beyond the scope of this article.
12. H.C. 731/86 *Microdaph Ltd v. The Electricity Company* 41(2) P.D. 449. Recently, the Knesset accepted the Administrative Courts Law, 2000. This statute provides that judicial review applications, appeals against administrative decisions and other administrative claims in the fields specified by the statute should be issued to the District Court, while the HCJ would serve as an appellate division for these matters. The new legislation, however, relates only to a limited number of fields, while preserving the function of the HCJ to serve as a trial court in all other fields of administrative controversies. Moreover, the new law provides that the HCJ is entitled to seize jurisdiction on every administrative action, even in the fields dealt with by the statute, if it decides to do so.
13. This structure of the judicial system where judicial review cases are referred directly to the Supreme Court is reminiscent of the judicial system formed during the colonial rule of the British Mandate in Palestine before the state of Israel was established. The purpose was that 'regular' disputes (i.e. in civil or criminal matters) would be adjudicated before the civil courts that were staffed by 'native' residents of Palestine. On the other hand, administrative cases, in which the Crown was involved, were designated directly to the Supreme Court that was staffed by judges of British origin (or those considered close enough to the regime). After the establishment of Israel the newly born state adopted the British judicial system (almost) in its entirety. During the first years after independence, and owing to the exigencies of security and economic pressures, no effort was made to effect comprehensive reform of the judicial system. After a few years, the HCJ acquired an enormous amount of prestige and public support. Therefore, any attempt on the part of the government to effect a change in its powers by introducing a reform in the judiciary would have been regarded as an attempt to infringe on the independence of the judiciary and on the principle of the rule of law. Thus, despite the clear shortcomings of this system from procedural point of view, no serious attempt was made to reform it. The powers and responsibilities of the HCJ were kept, by and large, in the same format as they have been since independence, subject only to some residual changes that were chiefly introduced by the rulings of the Court itself.
14. H.C. 935/89 *Ganor v. Attorney General* 44(2) P.D. 485; Zysblat, 'Protecting Fundamental Human Rights in Israel'.
15. Dotan, 'Judicial Rhetoric, Government Lawyers and Human Rights'.
16. Zysblat, 'Protecting Fundamental Human Rights in Israel'. The practice of the Committee to avoid publishing the names of the candidates for judicial appointment until after the Committee has made its decision was challenged in 1993 before the HCJ. The Court dismissed the petitions indicating that it found no reason to interfere with the practices of the Committee (H.C. 5771/93 *Zitrin v. Minister of Justice* 48(1) P.D. 661). Nevertheless, shortly after this decision the Committee reformed its practices to some extent, so that the names of candidates are currently published 21 days before the Committee discusses their candidacy.
17. The government was forced to back off after the appointment was challenged before the HCJ and after accusations in the media in relation to the legality of the decision. The matter soon entailed a huge public scandal that seriously endangered the stability of Netanyahu's government and ended up with criminal indictments against some senior government officials and politicians.
18. H.C. 11/79 *Mirkin v. Minister of Interior* 33(1) P.D. 502; H.C. 331/80 *Hatishbi v. Haron* 34(4) P.D. 113.
19. H.C. 287/69 *Meiron v. Minister of Employment* 24(1) P.D. 337; H.C. 348/70 *Kfir v. Religious Council of Ashkelon* 25(1) P.D. 685; H.C. 26/76 *Bar Shalom v. Zorea* 31(1) P.D. 796.

20. H.C. 561/75 *Ashkenazi v. Minister of Defence* 30(3) P.D. 309; H.C. 222/68 *Hugim Leumiem v. Minister of Police* 24(2) P.D. 141.
21. H.C. 46/50 *El Aiubi v. Minister of Defence* 4(1) P.D. 222.
22. H.C. 156/56 *Shor v. Attorney General* 11(1) P.D. 285; Y. Dotan, 'Should Prosecutorial Discretion Enjoy Special Treatment in Judicial Review? A Comparative Analysis of the Law in England and Israel', *Public Law* (1997), p.513.
23. Menachem Mautner, *The Decline of Formalism and the Rise of Values in Israeli Law*, Tel Aviv: Dyonon, 1994.
24. Y. Dotan, 'Does Israel Need a Constitutional Court', *Mishpat Umimshal (Law and Government)*, Vol. 5 (1999), p.117 (in Hebrew).
25. H.C. 910/86 *Ressler v. Minister of Defence* 42(2) P.D. 441, 477. While this wide concept of justiciability was not adopted in its entirety by all other justices of the Supreme Court, it did mark a willingness on the part of the Court substantially to widen the range of issues which were thereafter considered justiciable under the new approach.
26. H.C. 217/80 *Segal v. Minister of Interior* 34(4) P.D. 429, 443; H.C. 1/81 *Shiran v. Israeli Broadcasting Authority* 35(3) P.D. 365.
27. H.C. 910/86 *Ressler v. Minister of Defence* 42(2) P.D. 441; Mautner, *The Decline of Formalism*.
28. H.C. 389/80 *Dapei Zahav v. Broadcasting Authority* 35(1) P.D. 421; H.C. 376/81 *Lugasi v. Minister of Communications* 36(2) 449; H.C. 297/82 *Berger v. Minister of Interior* 37(3) P.D. 29; H.C. 987/94 *Euronet Kavei Zahav v. Minister of Communication* 48(5) P.D. 412; H.C. 5510/92 *Turkeman v. Minister of Defence* 42(8) P.D. 217; H.C. 3477/95 *Beb-Atie v. Minister of Education* 96(2) Takdin Elion 317; Zamir, 'Administrative Law'.
29. H.C. 680/88 *Schnitzer v. Chief Military Censor* 42(4) P.D. 617; H.C. 393/82 *Gama't Asachan v. Regional Commander of Judea and Samaria* 37(4) P.D. 785.
30. H.C. 329/81 *Nof v. Attorney General* 37(4) P.D. 326; Dotan, 'Should Prosecutorial Discretion Enjoy Special Treatment in judicial Review?'; H.C. 425/89 *Tsofan v. General Military Prosecutor* 43(4) P.D. 718; H.C. 935/89 *Ganor v. Attorney General* 44(2) P.D. 485; H.C. 7074/93 *Swissa v. Attorney General* 48(3) P.D. 749.
31. H.C. 6163/92 *Eizenberg v. Minister of Housing* 47(2) P.D. 229; H.C. 1284/99 *Ploni v. Chief of Staff* 53(2) P.D. 62.
32. H.C. 3094/93 *Movement for Government Quality v. Prime Minister* 47(5) P.D. 404; H.C. 4267/93 *Amitai v. Prime Minister* 47(5) P.D. 441.
33. H.C. 652/81 *Sarid v. Knesset Chairman* 36(2) P.D. 197; D. Kretzmer, 'Judicial Review of Knesset Decisions', *Tel Aviv Studies in Law*, Vol. 8 (1988), p.95.
34. The general practice of Israeli courts is to impose costs on the losing party on a 'no fault' basis. This practice, which is prevalent in civil law litigation, is less commonly implemented in litigation before the HCJ. Practitioners who often appear before the HCJ report that the Court refrains from imposing costs on petitioners in many cases of dismissals, and unless the petitioner has some 'fault' on her part. Such a fault may be related to misbehaviour during the process (such as failing to disclose an important fact to the Court), or an obstinate refusal to withdraw the petition despite suggestions on the part of the justices to do so. The Court is particularly slow to impose costs on the petitioner in cases where the petition, despite its dismissal, raised an important public issue; see Y. Dotan, 'Do the "Haves" still Come out Ahead? Bringing Activist Courts into the Picture', paper presented at the conference 'Do the "Haves" still Come out Ahead?' at the Institute of Legal Studies, University of Wisconsin Law School, Madison, Wisconsin, 1–2 May 1998.
35. Gad Barzilai, Ephraim Yuchtman-Ya'ar and Zeev Segal, *The Israeli Supreme Court and the Israeli Public*, Tel Aviv: Papyrus, 1993 (in Hebrew). The same authors also published the main findings in 'Supreme Court and Public Opinion: General Paradigms and the Israeli Case', *Law and Courts*, Vol. 3 (1994), p.3; Y. Dotan and M. Hofnung, 'Interest Groups in the High Court of Justice: Measuring Success in Litigation and in Out-of-Court Settlements', *Law and Policy*, Vol. 23, No.1 (2001), p.1; Y. Dotan and M. Hofnung, 'Legislators in Courts: The Judicial Politics of Israeli Political Parties', paper presented at the American Political Science Association Meeting, Boston, MA, 3–6 Sept. 1998. For example, of 822 petitions submitted before the High Court of Justice in 1980, only 12 (1.5 per cent), were filed by groups. The number of petitions filed by groups rose sharply to 40 in 1986 (4.4 per cent of 903 petitions). This trend continued well into the 1990s. In 1989, 59 petitions (5.6 per cent) were issued by groups. In 1991, of 1,069 files reviewed, 143 (13.4 per cent) were

filed by 72 different groups, and in 1993, of 1,208 files, 150 (12.4 per cent) were brought by 117 different groups. That rate was kept up in 1995 when, of 1,214 petitions reviewed, 151 (12.4 per cent) were issued by 102 groups; see Dotan and Hofnung, 'Interest Groups in the High Court of Justice'. Interest groups succeeded in challenging public policies and affecting government action through litigation in several cases during the last two decades. Among other instances, in cases eliminating censorship on theatre shows (H.C. 14/86 *Laor v. The Censorship Committee* 41(1) P.D 421); ordering the Ministry of the Interior to register as Jewish a woman who was converted to Judaism by a Reform Jewish rabbi in the US (H.C. 230/86 *Miller v. Minister of Interior* 40(3) P.D. 436); allowing for a hearing in decisions to demolish houses for security considerations in the Occupied Territories (H.C. 358/88 *Association for Civil Rights in Israel (ACRI) v. Commander of Central Command* 43(2) P.D. 529); forcing the attorney general to reconsider his decision not to file charges against the police chief inspector when the latter was allegedly involved in misconduct (H.C. 7074/93 *Swissa v. Attorney General* 48(3) P.D. 749); forcing the government to nominate more women on the boards of publicly owned companies (H.C. 453/94 *Women's Lobby v. Government of Israel* 48(5) P.D. 501); ordering the army to allow women to take the preliminary exams for entering a combat pilot course and enlist the ones who pass (H.C. 4541/94 *Miller v. Minister of Defence* 49(4) P.D. 94); striking down the government decision to fire the head of the civil service (H.C. 4446/96 *Movement for Quality Government v. Government of Israel* 1996 (3) Takdin Elion 443).
36. H.C. 3123/99-A *Hilman v. Minister for Internal Security* (11 May 1999, unreported); H.C. 3123/99-C *Hilman v. Minister for Internal Security* (7 July 1999, unreported).
37. Dotan, 'Judicial Rhetoric, Government Lawyers and Human Rights'.
38. Donald L. Horowitz, *The Courts and Social Policy*, Washington, DC: Brookings Institution, 1997, p.38.
39. The most prominent among these organizations are the Association for Civil Rights in Israel (ACRI); Hotline – The Centre for Human Rights, specializing in litigation concerning violations of human and civil rights in the Territories occupied by Israel after the Six-Day War of 1967; the Centre for Jewish Pluralism, concentrating on issues of freedom of religion; the Movement for Quality Government, an organization aimed at securing high standards of government officials and agencies (a judicial watch group); Man, Nature and Law, an environmental group.
40. The point may be illustrated by comparing the number of procedural regulations. The number of clauses included in the Code of Civil Procedure Regulations consists of over 500 different (and sometimes complex) clauses. The High Court of Justice Procedural Regulations is a short set of regulations containing no more than 23 clauses. Section 20(c) allows the Court to refer to the Code of Civil Procedure Regulations as complementary, but the Court seldom takes advantage of this option.
41. Denis J. Galligan, *Discretionary Powers*, Oxford: Oxford University Press, 1986; R.J. Pierce, 'Two Problems in Administrative Law: Political Polarity on the District of Columbia Circuit and Judicial Deterrence of Agency Rulemaking', *Duke Law Journal* (1988), p.300; Horowitz, *The Courts and Social Policy*, p.36; R.A. Kagan, 'Adversarial Legalism and American Government', *Journal of Policy Analysis and Management*, Vol. 10 (1991), p.369; Robert Baldwin and Christopher McCrudden, *Regulation in Public Law*, London: Weidenfeld and Nickolson, 1987; Joel F. Handler, *Social Movements and the Legal System*, New York: Academic Press, 1978.
42. Dotan, 'Judicial Rhetoric, Government Lawyers and Human Rights'.
43. The judicial activism of the HCJ has also wide implications on the private sector and the business community, since it affects economic regulation of the government. These implications are, however, beyond the scope of the current discussion.
44. Amnon Strachnov, *Justice under Fire*, Tel Aviv: Yedioth Ahronoth Books, 1994 (in Hebrew).

Choosing a Regulatory Regime: The Experience of the Israeli Electricity Market

MOSHE MAOR

INTRODUCTION

If there is a choice of institutional designs for the regulation of public utilities, how can such a choice be made between, for example, a single- or a multiple-industry regulator?[1] This question has become central to the debate about the running of industry in Israel in a way which would have been inconceivable only a few years ago. Until the 1990s, regulation was little discussed and there was little concern with designing institutions to undertake this task. Public ownership, it was assumed, should be the main means of importing public interest elements into the running of key industries and curbing their monopoly power. All this has changed with the gradual separation of enterprises from government control and privatization in such sectors as telecommunications and electricity. In so far as regulation is concerned, the creation in 1996 of an independent regulatory agency namely, the Public Utilities Authority – Electricity has been indicative of this change. The creation of other regulatory agencies in the natural gas sector, as well as in trains and railways, is currently in the early stages of legislation.

Despite the importance of this trend, little debate has taken place over the role of regulators and the design of regulatory institutions. The existing literature revolves around substantive regulatory decisions, such as the levels of price caps, the break-up of suppliers, and measures concerning competition (for example, interconnection terms). Yet, it is unlikely that agreement on substantive decisions can be reached between those involved in the utilities sector. If nothing else, there are conflicting interests among suppliers, and between suppliers' quest for profitability and consumers' demands for better service at the lowest possible cost. Besides, economists themselves tend to disagree about these matters. The lack of debate on the determinants of the constitutional and procedural aspects of regulation means that fundamental questions of how to design

Moshe Maor is Associate Professor of political science at the Hebrew University of Jerusalem.

regulatory institutions, why regulation takes place and what basic principles should be used by regulators have not yet been addressed.

To bridge this gap, this paper focuses on the design of the Public Utilities Authority – Electricity. Based on an institutional and historical analysis combined with interviews with public officials involved with the design of the electricity regulator, the paper analyses the ways that the Authority has interpreted the requirements set by law regarding accountability, transparency and procedural fairness. 'Accountability' is associated 'with the idea of "giving an account", that is, explaining or justifying actions, ideally in formal terms as in the case of a minister answering a question in parliament',[2] as well as with the idea of 'taking "into account" the consequences of one's actions for the welfare of others'.[3] 'Transparency' is defined as openness towards the public at large about an agency's structure, functions, policy intentions, accounts and projections. It involves ready access to reliable, comprehensive, timely, understandable and internationally comparable information on an agency's activities so that interested parties can accurately assess an agency's positions, true costs and benefits and present and future economic, social and political implications. 'Procedural fairness' refers to procedures or voluntary undertakings which enhance the regulator's claims to be acting properly (for instance, structured rule-making processes, hearings, and duties to give reasons).

The premise underlying the analysis is that there is no single right way to regulate. But there are a number of values that regulators need to satisfy if they wish to receive the approval of all parties concerned. Regulators should be, and should be seen to be, accountable, transparent and (procedurally) fair. If regulatory decisions fail to revolve around these values in the eyes of the regulated companies, their shareholders and employees, and especially their customers, who also constitute the national electorate, then whatever the substantive merits of such decisions, the subsequent regulation is unlikely to be successful.

The paper begins by exploring the theoretical lacuna in the field. It thereafter analyses the prominence, or the lack thereof, of accountability, transparency and procedural fairness in the Electricity Market Law 1996, and the regulatory experience gained so far. The derived institutional and procedural features of the Israeli regulatory regime in the electricity sector are then elaborated on, the preference for either a single- or multiple-industry regulator specified, and lessons for the Israeli regulatory regime drawn.

THEORETICAL BACKGROUND

The design of regulatory institutions has been a major concern of economists who tend to focus on the mechanisms available to regulators, most notably, pricing policies. Updated surveys of this literature have recently been provided by Kip, Vernon and Harrington.[4] Very little attention has been devoted to the study of the structure and design of regulatory agencies. Notable exceptions are the two competing approaches that focus on the relationship between regulatory agencies and their political principal. The notion that regulatory agencies follow the public interest is implicit in the first approach, which includes normative economic analyses of regulation.[5] An alternative view suggests that agencies are effectively constrained to follow their principals' goals.[6] Although both approaches are built on mechanisms for controlling the principal–agent problem that exists between the political actors who delegate regulatory authority to administrative agencies and the bureaucrats within those agencies, they fail to consider the design of regulatory institutions as exactly such a mechanism.

The works of Macey, and Spulber and Besanko go well beyond the above-mentioned approaches, and hence represent a genuine contribution to our understanding of the design of administrative agencies' procedures and organization.[7] Macey argues that since legislators delegate legislative power to administrative agencies that they themselves create, they can reduce the chances of possible administrative-agency deviation from the original intent by manipulating the structure and design of those agencies.[8] For example, should an agency be a single-industry regulator or should it regulate multiple industries? Macey's deduction is that when a single interest group dominates the legislative process (that is, during which an agency's structure and procedures are determined), 'the resulting administrative agency will be a single interest-group agency'.[9]

Spulber and Besanko take this logic a step further by looking at the implications for agency control in the US of three basic control instruments: appointments, statutes (namely, the extent of delegation), and supervision.[10] An important difference between these instruments is their timing. Appointments and statutes precede agency actions, while supervision can occur concurrent with or following agency decision-making, which implies differences in the level of information available to the decision-makers at the time of their respective actions. In terms of appointment and statute, these instruments show that if the agency cannot commit to a particular regulatory policy, the statute can be used to limit the discretion of the agency and the president can nominate an agency head whose preferences might significantly differ from those held by himself or herself. When the agency cannot commit to a particular regulatory policy, the potential for supervisory activity reduces the need to limit delegation. Thus, more active supervision may be seen in agencies with a wider statutory mandate.

The aforementioned studies indicate that our capacity to understand the ways in which institutions affect strategic opportunities over time, and in situations of incomplete information, has significantly increased over the past two decades mainly because of developments in game theory and in the economics of information. These studies, however, tell us very little about the incremental design of regulatory institutions (in other words, how the experience gained by the design of the first institution affects consecutive regulatory moves). An analysis of the Israeli experience of utility regulation gained so far will contribute to the accumulation of descriptive material aiding further theoretical development.

THE INSTITUTIONAL CONTEXT

Israel has a long tradition of operating its infrastructure industries as government-owned monopoly businesses. In the context of nation-building and under a severe security threat, Israeli governments have assumed a public responsibility for the provision of what they have regarded as essential infrastructure. The traditional approach has been for government departments to integrate planning, regulatory and operational functions into one package, utilizing the command powers of the state to obtain land and resources, employing statutes rather than contracts to facilitate actions, providing government guarantees on borrowing, and using access to consolidated revenue to fund losses. State departments of energy, for example, have had responsibility for approving development plans in the electricity infrastructure; the department of transportation (that is, the agency for public works) for developing the transportation infrastructure.

This structure has changed gradually as government businesses have moved from a bureaucratic to a commercial-style operation. A long-term trend has emerged towards more autonomy for enterprises and, for those capable of it, greater reliance on retained earnings as a source of profit. This trend has been clearly manifested in those sectors that have traditionally been protected but that operate in industries that are liberalized worldwide (for example, telecommunications, cable TV and air transportation). This trend has required, first and foremost, the formulation of principles for the introduction of competition into environments within which natural monopolies operate. Fundamental questions must be asked and answered. Should structural changes precede privatization? Which activities will remain under the public utility monopoly? How many firms will be allowed to operate in those sections that will be open for competition? What will be the rules of the game? Will the natural monopoly be allowed to privatize some of its activities without the approval of the government? Will the government sell shares to strategic investors, to the public, or to both? How will equal access to essential services be maintained? Why is regulation taking place? What basic principles should be used by regulators? The answers to these questions are critical in the process of designing regulatory institutions.

In the electricity market, the 70-year franchise of the Israel Electric Company (IEC) was about to expire in 1996. To prepare for this event, two public committees were commissioned in an attempt to answer some of the aforementioned questions: the Fogel Committee has focused mainly on a formula for tariff-setting,[11] and the Vardi Committee has dealt with the structural changes of the electricity market.[12] The former committee submitted its report in October 1991. It has recommended incorporating into statute the mechanism and the formula for the update of electricity tariffs, according to which control and monitoring of tariffs and prices will be conducted. Residual to its conclusions was a recommendation to set up a Public Utilities Commission (PUC), which would approve tariffs in agreement with the Finance Ministry; determine quality and reliability standards; shape modes of financial, technological and economic reporting; and determine parameters and standards for examination of the development plans produced by IEC. Additionally, it recommended that the PUC operation be transparent.[13]

The Vardi Committee submitted its report in December 1992. The committee avoided dealing with the structure of the electricity market, and recommended instead the introduction of competition in those market segments where competition can be introduced, and cautious regulation of those segments in which the natural monopoly must be retained. This was without specifying which segments should be open to competition and which should remain natural monopolies. The committee also introduced a 'tool-box' concept whereby the government is able to influence market structure via the allocation of licences. It thus recommended the licensing of IEC activities in a way that would enable a separation of different units on a functional and/or regional basis in the future in order to create a more competitive market structure. Licence provision and modification would be the responsibility of the Ministry of Energy and Infrastructure.

The Vardi Committee also recommended the creation of an independent PUC, which would regulate electricity tariffs and protect consumers. The PUC would be in charge of approving tariffs so that competition in the electricity market is improved; protecting consumers and defining the relationship between electricity providers and consumers; determining tariffs' principles and structure; designing standards for reliability and the level of service in the electricity market; and setting modes of reporting. In terms of regulatory procedures, the committee envisages the creation of a US-style agency, comprised of three to five members nominated for a five-year period. The agency would be granted quasi-judicial authority in those areas specified by law, but relevant parties would be able to challenge its decisions in court. Hearings would be conducted with all relevant parties. Funding would be provided by levies on licence-holders in the electricity sector in a way that guarantees the independence and autonomy of the PUC and its professional ability.[14]

The principles devised by the Fogel and Vardi committees were supposed to be transformed into actual policy options one of which would then be transformed into draft legislation. This task has been entrusted to Daniel Czamanski of the Technion. A special budget of two million NIS was allotted in the 1993 state budget to cover costs related to this task. Numerous reports have been produced by Czamanski's team. In Czamanski's final report (entitled 'interim report'), three principles have been devised: (1) natural monopolies must be retained in segments of the IEC's activities where there is economic and technical justification for doing so; (2) competition must be introduced into all other segments (that is, when no economic or technical justification exists for the retention of a natural monopoly); and (3) regulation must be introduced in segments where a natural monopoly is retained. Specifically, a natural monopoly will be preserved in electricity transmission; competition will be introduced into the generation segment; and four regional distribution firms will be created.[15]

Given that the 'reform clock' in Israel is ticking in four-year intervals, Czamanski had either to work faster or to produce a non-drastic recommendation. As he failed to do both, the recommendation to incorporate the aforementioned principles in the electricity market law was rejected by the then minister of energy, Moshe Shahal. In other words, reforms that would have been acceptable in 1993 proved to be non-viable in the run-up to the 1996 election. The rejection of Czamanski's recommendation has implied an end to drastic reform, as occurred in the UK. What emerges is rather an incremental process of reform.

The subsequent Electricity Market Law 1996 specified only that the licence of the Israeli Electric Company, which enjoys statutory protection of its monopoly position, would expire in 2006, and that 20 per cent of electricity production will be gradually transferred to private firms, 10 per cent to local producers and 10 per cent to producers from neighbouring countries. In addition, no clear statement has been provided as to the areas that will remain under the monopoly of the IEC, the areas that will be opened up for competition, the number of firms that will be allowed in, and the rules of the game. An internal document setting out these principles was designed by the Ministry of Finance, the Ministry of National Infrastructure and the Government Companies Authority only in October 1998.[16] So far, this document has not been made public.

THE DEMOCRATIC DEFICIT OF THE PUBLIC UTILITY AUTHORITY – ELECTRICITY

With the decision that the IEC's licence would expire in 2006 came the establishment of an industry-specific regulatory office: the Public Utilities Authority – Electricity. The regulatory framework and the duties of the regulator were provided for in the Electricity Market Law 1996. Under this law, companies wishing to operate in the electricity market are required to have a licence, which is granted by the minister of energy and infrastructure.[17] The minister has also been given sole responsibility in respect of licence modification and violations of licence instructions.

The Public Utilities Authority – Electricity has a very short list of duties, powers and functions. These include '(1) setting tariffs and methods for their update, and (2) setting standards for level, quality of service provided by the licensee of the essential service ... and control of the fulfillment of the obligations according to the standards'.[18] In addition, 'The Authority will check consumers' complaints'.[19]

In considering the aforementioned duties of the Authority, one feature is particularly striking: the tasks are very broad, thus leaving the regulator with a great deal of discretion. Take, for example, the way in which the Authority's tasks should be executed. In an attempt to challenge the Authority's decision on a price review in the High Court of Justice, the IEC claimed that the Authority's double tasks (that is, setting tariffs and setting standards) could be seen as integrated with each other and, in practice, as two sides of an equation: setting electricity tariffs that are based on quality standards determined by the Authority. Electricity tariffs should thus be set according to the level of services required from the licence-holder, which the Authority must determine parallel to electricity tariffs. The law further specifies that, 'The Authority will set standards, subject to the development plans approved by the Minister according to Clause 19; the standards will be viewed by the public and be published in a way determined by the Minister'.[20] This clause means, according to the IEC, that the quality standards provided by the IEC, and according to which tariffs' setting take place, are derived in accordance with, and subject to, the development plans approved by the minister. The sequence that emerges is the approval of development plans by the minister, the setting of standards thereafter, and lastly, the setting of tariffs on the basis of the aforementioned standards.

However, the law did not impose restrictions on the Authority's discretion in so far as the execution of its narrow mandate is concerned. According to this view, the Authority enjoys a great deal of discretion in all matters related to tariffs and standards-setting. The aforementioned example illustrates precisely this leverage: the authority is not obliged to set standards before tariffs. It could rely on existing 'Instructions for

Providing Electricity to Consumers' in setting its tariffs until new standards are devised. Doing so does not violate Clause 33, as the IEC's development plans are based on existing instructions for providing electricity.

The IEC's attempts to challenge in the courts substantive decisions regarding the sequence of tariff-setting, determination of the efficiency factor, setting acceptable rates of return on capital, and the implementation of the cost principle in determining tariffs, has ended in failure. The High Court of Justice did not delve into the economic analysis of the aforementioned matters, rather, it based its decision on the view that the Authority is the only body allowed by statute to decide these matters.

The great deal of discretion enjoyed by the Authority has been, indeed, in line with the regulatory philosophy of the Ministry of Finance.[21] The aim was to balance the many competing interests involved in utility regulation and to deal with the changing nature of the sector. Moreover, it was an essential part of its independence from control either by elected politicians or by judges. Nevertheless, underlying the regulatory philosophy of the Ministry of Finance has been the need of the Authority to strike a balance between it enjoying discretion, and ensuring that discretion is not excessive and is exercised transparently.

Regarding transparency, Shlomo Brovender head of electricity administration in the Ministry of National Infrastructures and the ministry's chief initiator of the Electricity Market Law 1996 thought transparency in the IEC's activities would help the regulator detect gross inefficiencies such as hidden unemployment, contracts awarded without tenders or on the basis of nepotism or other particularistic considerations.[22] Ran Mosenson, chief adviser on utility regulation in the Ministry of Finance during the formative phase of legislation, had a much broader interpretation of the transparency requirement somewhat resembling the model of Oftel.[23] The idea was for the regulator to be as open as possible in the discussion of issues arising out of its functions and duties, and to have straightforward provision of information. In procedural terms, it implies an annual operating plan setting out objectives, priorities and a US-style regulative programme that includes making public statements about issues under review, establishing contact with individuals, companies and representative bodies with interests in the field, and becoming fully aware of their views. It would also provide the most complete explanation possible regarding the basis of its decisions, subject only to the need to respect commercial confidentiality. It would facilitate the preparation of consultation documents to which representations are invited and make public those representations made during consultation, except when the director general is requested not to do so. Finally it would establish a website containing consultative documents, responses to them and other information.[24]

These procedures provide an opportunity for an exchange of views by participants through a consultation procedure and public hearings, as well as for moving from a passive receipt of information by the regulator to the encouragement of an active debate among interested parties and a response to them in successive papers. These procedures also enable a move away from reliance on hearings that provide sporadic references on a case-by-case basis and towards an approach establishing principles on matters of how to approach the evaluation of an acceptable rate of return on capital, efficiency factor, the asset base and cost of capital, which could be used later on by other regulators.

The Electricity Market Law 1996 does not contain detailed provisions as to the issue of transparency. It does not provide any specification as to the transparency of data and decision-making processes, but does require interested parties to be invited to air their claims, and the publication of decisions and the reasons underlying them. Clause 33 specifies that, 'The Authority will set standards, subject to the development plan approved by the Minister ...; The standards will be made public and be published in a way determined by the Minister'. Clause 36 further indicates that 'The Authority's decisions according to this law, including explanations regarding the methods of tariff setting and statistical data, will be made public, except if the Authority decides differently in special circumstances for specific reasons which will be made public'. Regarding the incorporation of other interested parties into the decision-making process, Clause 37 specifies that, 'For the fulfillment of its tasks ... the Authority will allow representatives of consumer groups to bring propositions and policy stances before it regarding tariffs and standard setting, in a way determined by the Minister, in consultation with the Finance Minister, according to the Authority's proposal'.

Thus, data and decision-making processes within the Authority are secretive; tariffs are set behind closed doors between the chairman of the Authority and its board on the basis of the inputs produced by the Authority's professional departments. There is more reliance on works produced by private consultants than by professionals from academia or industry who enjoy worldwide reputations. Consultants' papers or summaries of these reports are not made public. Although much weight is given to consultants' advice, no opportunity to debate such advice is given. Only the regulated company may have full access to some parts of the reports as it must confront their conclusions in hearings that take place behind closed doors. Other participants in the price review process do not have full access to consultants' reports. This may be justified when there are strong reasons of commercial confidentiality, but not in situations when such reasons do not apply.

Furthermore, interested parties can ask for protocols of the Authority's meetings, but they will get only those parts that have substantial and direct relation to the decision, not the 'way of thinking' which led to it. Thus, there is no way of testing how the Authority is using the evidence supplied to it to come to a decision.

Had the decision-making process been transparent, it would have been understandable for representatives of the minister of finance and of the minister of national infrastructure to have a seat in the four-member board of the Authority. Had the decision-making process been transparent, it would have been understandable for the minister of finance and the minister of national infrastructure (formerly energy and infrastructure) to send separate letters addressed to the Public Utilities Authority – Electricity, expressing their views on aspects under the sole responsibility of the Authority.[25] The fact that the ministers and public officials involved were not invited by the Authority to air their claims places a big question mark on the attempts by the minister of finance and the minister of national infrastructure to influence Authority's decisions.

The requirement by law to publish new tariffs has been fulfilled so far, except for a decision by the Authority in a meeting held on 4 June 1997, during which a decision was taken for a 0.6 per cent increase in the average electricity price. This decision was not made public, rather it became valid on 12 June 1997 (without prior public notification) with the routine update of electricity tariffs and a series of changes within the structure of tariffs.[26] This illustrates again the very narrow interpretation by the Authority of the transparency requirements set by the law.

Regarding accountability, the 'founding fathers' of the regulatory regime in the Israeli electricity market had numerous options. Utility regulators could have been accountable to parliament via parliamentary committee or ministerial guidelines, to government via cost–benefit testing of regulation or via share ownership, to monitoring or appeal bodies, to a super agency, to judges and to consumers. Utility regulators could have been required to publish statements of objectives, give reasons for decisions, provide wider disclosure of information, conduct public hearings or utilize structured rule-making processes in order to balance and protect disparate interests. Apart from the degree of information made public concerning the regulator's operation, consultative documents and responses to them, utility regulators could have utilized a variety of communication channels, such as a site on the Internet.

On the face of it, the list of controls over the Public Utility Authority – Electricity is impressive. According to the Electricity Market Law 1996, the director of the Public Utilities Commission – Electricity is appointed by the government (on the basis of a recommendation by the finance minister and the energy and infrastructure minister) for a limited, but renewable, term and may be dismissed on grounds of incapacity or misbehaviour. The Authority also falls under the responsibility of the State Comptroller's Office, which scrutinizes the economy and efficiency of its operations. The latter has the power to investigate any injustice which results from misadministration. In addition, the Public Utilities Commission and its members can only act within the terms of their statutory roles and are therefore subject to supervision by the courts on the grounds of illegality or procedural impropriety.

In substantive matters, however, the system of accountability that emerges is relatively weak. Most important, on matters related to tariffs and standards-setting, judicial challenges cannot be mounted unless procedures specified by law are not followed. On administrative matters, the law provides for only intermittent and irregular scrutiny; it is limited in its scope and uncertain in outcome since it lacks realistic sanctions. The Public Utilities Authority – Electricity manifests, therefore, a very weak form of accountability on substantial aspects of its operations.

It is reasonable to conclude that, in so far as accountability, transparency and procedural fairness are concerned, the Authority's interpretation of the law is only remotely a reflection of what was hoped for by its framers. The pillar underlying the Ministry of Finance's philosophy has been a great deal of discretion over the regulatory tasks, combined with control over these activities by the demands for transparency and accountability. A loosely prescribed regulatory regime that relies heavily upon the regulator's discretion indicates that an essential element of the Ministry of Finance's advice in the formative stage of the legislation (for example, regarding the Oftel model) is missing. Consequently, much of the operational detail needed to build a functioning regulatory system has to be established *in situ* by the regulators themselves. This fault has been a source of many bitter conflicts between the Authority and the rest of the actors involved in the electricity markets.

SINGLE- VS. MULTIPLE-INDUSTRY REGULATORS

In theory, the case for a multiple-industry utilities commission may appear relatively solid. Very few would object to a body that brings existing and new regulators under one roof with the aim of promoting policy consistency between them. Thus, there may be a strong case for merging the electricity and natural gas regulators into a single office for energy regulation, which could also take over a number of regulatory functions for the water industry. A similar argument may be applied to transport, rail and airport regulators, as well as to communications and broadcasting. In practice, however, this conclusion is far from being decisive. In fact, the Israeli experience of utility regulation suggests the opposite conclusion. When one considers the lack of balance that exists between the great deal of discretion enjoyed by the Authority over tariffs and standards-setting, on the one hand, and its weak transparency and accountability, on the other, it appears that an attempt should be made to modify the Electricity

Market Law 1996, as well as to avoid the diffusion of such a problematic culture to other regulatory institutions. Thus, the clear recommendation which emerges is to modify the design of single-industry regulators.

The Public Utilities Authority – Electricity has been given limited but precise duties that are separate from those of the government. It has also been required to give reasons for its decisions. However, it has failed to balance its heavy reliance on outside consultants in recent price reviews, on the one hand with the opportunity to debate consultants' views, on the other. The lack of access by other participants to either consultants' reports or their summaries supports the accusation that the Authority lacks a full commitment to transparency and accountability.

This problem might be resolved by periodic governmental and parliamentary reviews of regulatory performance. However, this solution contradicts the intention of the framers of the regulatory regime who emphasized the need to neutralize political interventions. Another possible suggestion is to set up an appeal or arbitration procedure. However, without a set of principles on the opening of the electricity market to competition and the derived regulatory guidance, such a solution will be no more than a process of a second-guessing the regulator.

A reasonable proposal which emerges is that the Authority should have a statutory duty to issue an annual 'Document of Principles' which sets out its overall view of the implications of its statutory duties on the state of IEC and the electricity sector at large in financial and operational terms. Furthermore, if a decision of the Authority is judicially reviewed, inconsistency between the decision in question and the Document would offer evidence in support of a challenge to that decision. Thus the Document would provide greater transparency, accountability and predictability.

Another reasonable recommendation is that the Authority should facilitate consultation documents upon which representations are invited; make public representations during consultation, except when the need arises for commercial confidentiality; and establish a homepage on the Internet containing consultative documents, responses to them and other information.

Finally, the lack of clear-cut transparency and accountability provisions in the Electricity Market Law 1996 was a mistake. The reliance on a framework law which allows for flexibility and a great deal of regulatory discretion has been another mistake that led to vagueness and unpredictability in the operation of the regulator. The light-handed approach implemented in the formulation of the Electricity Market Law 1996 emphasizes the urgent need for regulatory reform. Without it, problematic decisions taken at the time of privatization will continue to determine the parameters within which the electricity regulator works.

NOTES

The author thanks the KORET Fund for financial support. He also thanks those who agreed to be interviewed for their help: Shlomo Brovender, head of electricity administration at the Ministry of National Infrastructure, Moshe Tzur, head of the economic department at the Public Utilities Authority – Electricity, Dana Giorini, head of the legal department at the Public Utilities Authority – Electricity, Yishai Dror, formerly an adviser to the Finance Ministry and the Public Utilities Authority – Electricity, and Daniel Czamanski. The author also acknowledges the comments by Reuven Groneau. Of course, only the author can be held responsible for the analysis and interpretation presented here.

1. Single-industry regulators can be found in the UK, Italy (communications and energy) and Israel (electricity). The British regulatory regime, for example, was established under a series of statutes. Under these Acts, industry-specific regulators were created, each headed by a director general (DG): Oftel (the Office of Telecommunication, headed by the director general of telecommunications), Ofgas (the Office of Gas Supply, headed by the director general of gas supply), Offer (the Office of Electricity Regulation, headed by the director general of electricity supply), and Ofwat (the Office of Water Services, headed by the director general of water services). Multiple-industry regulators (i.e., utilities commissions) are found in the US and Canada. In the former, for example, there is a long history of agencies at the federal level, such as the Federal Communications Commission regulating telecommunication and broadcasting. The procedures of these bodies are governed by the Administrative Procedure Act, which grants important protections in terms of both rule-making and adjudication. At the state level, many states have public service commissions that regulate utilities; thus, for example, the New York Public Service Commission regulates power and gas utilities, telecommunications, and water companies. The commissions are governed by state legislation, such as the New York Public Service Law, and by some federal legislation, notably the Public Utility Regulatory Policies Act.
2. B. Stone, 'Administrative Accountability in the 'Westminster' Democracies: Towards a New Conceptual Framework', *Governance*, Vol. 8, No. 4 (1995), p.508.
3. J.D. Donahue, *The Privatization Decision: Public Ends, Private Means*, New York, Basic Books, 1989, p.10.
4. V. Kip, J.M. Vernon and J.E. Harrington Jr, *Economics of Regulation and Antitrust*, 2nd edn, Cambridge, MA, The MIT Press, 1997.
5. M. Bernstein, *Regulating Business by Independent Commission*, Princeton, NJ, Princeton University Press, 1955; S. Kelman, 'Occupational Safety and Health Administration', in J.Q. Wilson (ed.), *The Politics of Regulation*, New York, Basic Books, 1980, pp.236–66; G.J. Stigler, 'The Theory of Economic Regulation', *Bell Journal of Economics*, Vol. 6 (1971), pp.3–21; W. Niskanen, *Bureaucracy and Representative Government*, Chicago, Aldine, 1971. For an extensive review of this literature see R. Noll, 'Government Regulatory Behavior: A Multidisciplinary Survey and Synthesis', in R.G. Noll (ed.), *Regulatory Policy and the Social Sciences*, Berkeley, CA, University of California Press, 1985.
6. B.R. Weingast, 'The Congressional-Bureaucratic System: A Principal–Agent Perspective with Application to the SEC', *Public Choice*, Vol. 44 (1984), pp.147–92; B.R. Weingast and M.J. Moran, 'Bureaucratic Discretion or Congressional Control: Regulatory Policymaking by the Federal Trade Commission', *Journal of Political Economy*, Vol. 91 (1983), pp.765–800.
7. J.R. Macey, 'Organizational Design and the Political Control of Administrative Agencies', *The Journal of Law, Economics and Organization*, Vol. 8, No. 1 (1992), pp.93–110; D.F. Spulber and D. Besanko, 'Delegation, Commitment, and the Regulatory Mandate', *The Journal of Law, Economics and Organization*, Vol. 8, No. 1 (1992), pp.126–54.
8. Macey, 'Organizational Design'.
9. Macey, 'Organizational Design', p.100.
10. Spulber and Besanko, 'Delegation, Commitment, and the Regulatory Mandate'.
11. Ministry of Finance, *Report of the Committee for the Examination of Electricity Tariffs*, Jerusalem, Government Press, 1991 (The Fogel Committee).
12. Ministry of Finance and Ministry of Energy and Infrastructure, *Report of the Committee for the Examination of Israel Electric Company's Franchise*, Jerusalem, Government Press, 1992 (The Vardi Committee).
13. Ministry of Finance, *Report of the Committee for the Examination of Electricity Tariffs*.

14. Ministry of Finance and Ministry of Energy and Infrastructure, *Report of the Committee for the Examination of Israel Electric Company's Franchise.*

15. Ministry of Energy and Infrastructure, *Public Utilities Authority – Electricity: An Interim Report,* Jerusalem, 1994 (Czamanski's report, unpublished); Ministry of Energy and Infrastructure, 'The Israeli Electricity Market in Israel – Reorganization', Jerusalem, Ministry of Energy and Infrastructure, July 1994. Another report provided a detailed scheme of the Authority's structure, duties and guiding principles. A number of principles that the Authority will act upon are: non-discrimination among customers, encouraging efficiency, improving competition in the electricity market, and transparency of data and processes. See Ministry of Energy, 'Organizational Structure and Working Processes of the PUC', June 1994 (report written by O. Gloskinus and A.J. Amiad, unpublished).

16. Amiram Cohen, 'A Document Setting the Principle for the Opening of Electricity Sector for Competition Has Been Designed', *Ha'aretz,* 26 Oct. 1998.

17. Seven projects to set up private power plants, producing in the range of 5 to 50 megawatts of electricity, were approved in the National Framework Plan for Small Private Power Plants 10. The government, however, has yet to approve the continuation of these plants' build-up. Objections by local residents and environmental bodies, changing political circumstances and power struggles between the two ministries involved are being blamed for the delay in government approval. The importance of these power plants lies in their being part of the process of privatizing the electricity market, the introduction of market forces, and the simultaneous breaking-up of the monopoly of the Israeli Electric Company.

18. The Electricity Market Law 1996, 30(1), (2).

19. The Electricity Market Law 1996, 37(1), (2).

20. Ibid.

21. R. Mosenson, 'Public Utilities Regulation', unpublished document, Budget Unit, Ministry of Finance, Oct. 1991; R. Mosenson, 'Electricity Tariff for IPPs: Regulation vs. "Market Solution". Orientation of the Structural–Functional Reform of the Electricity Market', unpublished document, Budget Unit, Ministry of Finance, Oct. 1993; R. Mosenson, 'Costs and Tariffs in the Electricity Network', unpublished document, Budget Unit, Ministry of Finance, April 1994; R. Mosenson, 'The Structure of the Electricity Sector and its Operation – A Clarification Document', unpublished document, Budget Unit, Ministry of Finance, Sept. 1994; R. Mosenson, 'A Framework Proposal for the Public Utilities Authority – Electricity', unpublished document, Budget Unit, Ministry of Finance, July 1995; R. Mosenson, 'The Electricity Law: Necessary Contents', unpublished document, Budget Unit, Ministry of Finance, Jan. 1995; R. Mosenson, 'Inputs for a Working Paper for a PUC', unpublished document, Budget Unit, Ministry of Finance, Dec. 1996; R. Mosenson and Y. Dror, 'A Framework Proposal for the Public Utilities Authority – Electricity', unpublished document, Budget Unit, Ministry of Finance, Aug. 1996.

22. Interview with Shlomo Brovender, Nov. 1998, Jerusalem.

23. I. Maoz, 'Dr Ran Mosenson – A Profile', *The Public Utility Authority – Electricity,* a report, Jerusalem, Public Utility Authority – Electricity, May 1999; R. Mosenson, 'A Framework Proposal for the Public Utilities Authority – Electricity', unpublished document, Budget Unit, Ministry of Finance, July 1995; R. Mosenson, 'The Electricity Law: Necessary Contents', unpublished document, Budget Unit, Ministry of Finance, Jan. 1995; R. Mosenson, 'Inputs for a Working Paper for a PUC', unpublished document, Budget Unit, Ministry of Finance, Dec. 1996

24. T. Prosser, *Law and the Regulators,* Oxford: Clarendon Press, 1997.

25. Letter from Yaakov Neeman, minister of finance, addressed to Prof. Haim Elata, chairman, Public Utilities Authority – Electricity, dated 16 Sept. 1997; Letter from Ariel Sharon, minister of national infrastructure, addressed to Prof. Haim Elata, chairman, Public Utilities Authority – Electricity, dated 16 Sept. 1997.

26. An internal memorandum written by Ran Mosenson, Ministry of Finance, 26 June 1997.

The Role of State and Public Audit in Safeguarding Ethics in the Public Service: Whose Ethics? What Ethics?

ASHER FRIEDBERG

THE LEGAL AND CONTENT INFRASTRUCTURE: AMBIGUITIES AND COMPLEXITIES

One of the audit standards according to which the state comptroller of Israel examines audited bodies is the moral integrity standard. This standard is unique among other audit standards – such as legality, orderly management, efficiency, economy and effectiveness – mentioned in the State Comptroller Law. This is not only because of the ambiguity surrounding it, but because it is considered a dynamic standard, into which the state comptroller 'pours' content and for which he designs ethical norms. That's why the state comptroller is considered to be the arbiter of moral integrity in the public service, and not only in Israel.[1] The second state comptroller of Israel, the late Dr Nebenzhal, noted that, 'The role of moral integrity in state audit, firmly based in the State Comptroller Law and in actual practice, has had a strong influence on the status of the state comptroller. He is seen as the public service's moral guide.' And he added, 'Mentioning a finding concerning moral integrity in a report given on an audited entity is seen by the public, and especially by the audited entity itself, as a severe rebuke that can't be ignored.'[2] One can say that the activities of the state comptroller based on this standard turn him into a public service ethics shaper, an activist auditor.[3]

The state comptroller's duty to examine infringements on moral integrity is mentioned five times in the state audit laws. Section 2(b) of the Basic Law: The State Comptroller, enacted in 1988, states: 'The State Comptroller shall examine the legality, moral integrity, orderly management, efficiency and economy of the inspected bodies.' The State Comptroller Law, 5718-1958 (Consolidated Version) refers to this duty in

Asher Friedberg is Professor and the Director of the Graduate Programme in Public and Internal Auditing in the Department of Political Science at Haifa University.

section 10(a)(2), which deals with the extent of inspection; in section 14(a) and (b) which deals with audit results; and in section 15, which concerns the annual report on government offices and state institutions.

The professional literature refers to scholars' notes that suggest that the Hebrew combination of the words 'moral integrity' – *tohar hamidot*, which means, literally, the purity of standards – is not of biblical origin, but rather a twentieth-century attempt to express the idea of moral integrity. It did not appear in the original version of the State Comptroller Law of 1949, but was included in the amendments to the law in 1952. Nebenzhal points out that this 'foggy' expression was shaped as a 'concept of practical ethics, pointing to positive and even lofty qualities. This expression evokes a positive emotional reaction, just like offences concerning moral integrity evoke negative emotional approaches'.[4]

It seems that there are enough grounds to conclude that the term 'moral integrity' is vague, ambiguous and difficult to define. It could be placed somewhere between criminal acts and infringements on orderly management. In this context, and adding to the confusion, it should be mentioned that the official English translation of the State Comptroller Laws refers to this term in one place as 'morally irreproachable manner' and in another as an 'infringement on moral standards'.

Examining ethical issues in the various sectors of the public administration system in accordance with the moral integrity standard has to be carried out by the state comptroller in all of the entities audited by him. It is difficult to sum up the number of entities subject to audit by the state comptroller. Given the fact that the public sector in Israel is one of the largest among Western democratic states, we refer to approximately 1,000 entities located in the centre and margins of the public sector, maybe more, that are subject to audit by the state comptroller: government ministries and agencies, local authorities, government and public enterprises, and many other sub-sectors and types of bodies.[5] Given this vast web of entities, it is not surprising that the state comptroller constantly reveals in his annual reports, as well as in other reports, infringements on moral integrity.

In reference to the scope and complexity of the public administration system in Israel, it should be emphasized that the use of the moral integrity standard by the state comptroller is not disassociated from the web of social and institutional factors, and the enduring tension that exists in the governmental and administrative systems and sub-systems between the public and the private interest. This tension could be a fertile ground for events that deviate from normative rules and principles defined by the state comptrollers as infringements on moral integrity. The Israeli background, in this context, is characterized by some factors that 'donate' to the appearance of such infringements. The most visible are: the massive involvement of administration in all facets of daily life; the numerous areas of friction that have developed between the government and the citizen; the lack of service standards in the bureaucracy and the consequent conviction of many citizens that the only way to get service is with the aid of protekzia or worse; the difficulties of an immigrant society; the deep socio-economic/ethnic divisions in Israeli society, with some sectors which look upon government as the enemy and who consider diverting public funds to their own use perfectly acceptable, whatever the moral improprieties involved; the high level of politicization in the public service, which creates expectations of the advancement of personal interests, contrary to the public interest. And on top of it all the prominence of 'personal example' problems projected by high-ranking officials – elected and nominated – in the public administration system in Israel.

In reference to these factors, the state comptroller's task was, and is, to decide in each relevant case if there has been an infringement on moral integrity and the criteria for these decisions, taking into account that there is no clear definition of 'moral integrity', on the one hand, and thus that there is a necessity to decide what an infringement on moral integrity is, on the other hand. It means that the comptroller has to mould, in each case, clear and acceptable patterns of moral integrity. On this matter, the former state comptroller (and former Supreme Court justice), Miriam Ben-Porath, mentions another 'foggy' expression related to the judicial procedure – 'breach of trust'. Justice Ben-Porath cites a verdict concerning this expression: 'The legislature used an undefined expression. There are, of course, some advantages to it because it allows one to cast contents in this expression according to changes in the circumstances of life. On the other hand, there are some disadvantages – the casting of the contents is done after the occurrence of the event.'[6]

APPROACHES OF STATE COMPTROLLERS TO ETHICAL ISSUES

Another interesting question for examination concerns the approaches of state comptrollers to ethical issues. It seems that the personality of a state comptroller, on the one hand, and the accumulation of phenomena that seem to be infringements on moral integrity, on the other hand, can sometimes lead to a cardinal change in the approach of a state comptroller to such phenomena. The issue of political appointments is a good example. Until the end of the 1980s, not one of the state comptrollers referred to this issue. The fourth state comptroller, Justice Maltz, mentioned it only marginally at the end of his term of office. It is well known that this phenomenon was rooted, with different degrees of intensity, in the various sectors of the public administration system in Israel. It is also clear that this phenomenon contributed extensively to the corruption of the public administration system in Israel and that its scope was exceptional compared to similar phenomena in other Western countries.[7] Therefore, it is surprising that the state comptrollers did not refer to it until 1989. Moreover, this phenomenon, which was definitely far from being a secret to the state comptrollers, was not defined as even a minor irregularity, not to mention an infringement on moral integrity. Suddenly, in 1989, this phenomenon became an infringement on moral integrity and public ethics, a severely corrupt activity, a deviation from the law that projects negatively on the whole public sector, and demands legal and administrative reforms to cope with it. In 1998, the state comptroller extended his audit and referred to political appointments in the local government sector, too.[8]

The fact that the personality of the state comptrollers in Israel is an important factor in shaping the approaches, and the concepts, of the state audit institution to ethical dilemmas in the public sector was mentioned previously. It should be emphasized that whenever we refer to shaping and designing approaches and concepts of the state audit institution we mean, in practical terms, that this is being done by the state comptroller, who is the head of this institution.

The law in Israel that regulates this institution is not the State Audit Institution Law but the State Comptroller Law, which is not the case concerning the Internal Audit Law (and not the Internal Auditor Law). The state comptroller undersigns each report. The concepts, approaches and emphases expressed in the reports are his. He is responsible, personally, for their contents, and decides even upon their wording, phrasing. Thereby the Israeli state comptroller joins many other state comptrollers in the world who, in a way, personify state auditing in their countries. This system is contrary to the chamber approach in state auditing, according to which several auditors combine to form a joint audit body.

There are several explanations as to why some ethical issues that were 'excluded' from the audit subjects list by some state comptrollers in Israel, suddenly became 'hot' audited issues by others. One explanation is the expansion of phenomena that are considered to be infringements on moral integrity. It became impossible to accept these infringements. In the case of political appointments, one can point to the vast growth of the central committees (*merkazim*) of the political parties during the 1980s. Hundreds of the central committee members would appeal to the ministers of their parties asking for appointments, especially before elections. Findings of the state comptroller point clearly to the massive expansion of this phenomenon.[9]

Another explanation has to do with the personal approaches of the state comptrollers to certain occurrences related to moral integrity. Up until 1988, certain state comptrollers did not consider, from the state auditing point of view, political appointments to be infringements on moral integrity. They may have felt that this issue was beyond the scope of their authority; or, possibly, they simply believed that they were not strong enough to take on the political machine behind this practice.

Moreover, it could be that some state comptrollers considered that dealing with 'delicate' issues such as political appointments was potentially harmful to the respected status and position that the state audit institution had gained over the years.

My conclusion is that the state comptroller's personality (on the scale between passive and active), his outlook, his character and his functioning have an impact on his decisions to audit issues and entities that were not audited in the past in general, and issues of moral integrity and ethics, in particular. The former state comptroller, Justice Ben-Porath, was characterized by her activist approach, her style and her ability to expand the state audit successfully to new domains, including highly sensitive issues as moral integrity and public service ethics in the Israeli administrative system.

PUBLIC SERVICE ETHICS – WHOSE ETHICS? WHAT ETHICS?

An examination and analysis of a series of events that were defined as 'infringements on moral integrity' by the state comptroller since the establishment of the state audit institution can help identify the patterns of this phrase and reveal some aspects of the reaction of the public service to it.

The two basic questions that are inherent and intertwined, from the state comptroller's point of view, in the phrases 'public service ethics' and 'moral integrity' are: Whose ethics? What ethics? These questions bring us back to the state comptroller's *Annual Report No. 4* (1953), which was the first report that dealt substantially with the aforementioned dilemmas. The report presented the basic concept of the state comptroller as it was understood then. It discussed the place and roles of the state audit institution in examining ethical issues in the Israeli public service as stated in the amendment of the State Comptroller Law (July 1952), which included among the state comptroller's duties the examination of moral integrity of the audited entities.

In the aforementioned report and in the one that followed it, No. 5 (1954), the state comptroller struggled with such problems as: 'What is the meaning of this additional duty? How is it possible to inspect the adherence to moral standards? What does moral integrity demand and what can be done to maintain and strengthen it?' These struggles continued to accompany the state comptroller in the first years of his activities, reiterating the need for clear, normative standards in the public service that would help prevent infringements on moral integrity in the public service ('An open door may tempt a saint.'). Against this background, at the state comptroller's initiative, a special commission was set up by the Israeli Political Science Association to suggest norms of behaviour for public officials. It published its findings and recommendations in 1958, many of which remain valid to this day.

Geist and Friedberg[10] mention a survey carried out in 1991 by students of state audit at Haifa University, which dealt with 91 cases of infringements (or fear of infringements) on norms of moral integrity during the period 1953–88. (1) Among 50 cases relating to central government ministries and institutions, eight dealt with the Ministry of Housing, eight with the Ministry of Agriculture, five with the Ministry of Defence, four with the Ministry of Education and four with the Ministry of Health. Forty-one cases were related to local government, public corporations and other audited bodies. (2) In 39 cases, there was no indication of anything being done about these infringements, in the reports themselves, in the government's responses to the reports, or in follow-up reports of the state comptroller. In 48 cases, the responsible minister dealt with the infringement, while the remainder were handled by the Civil Service Commission and the police. (3) In 64 cases, new regulations were issued or old ones were amended. In 17 cases there was no indication of any change in the rules, while in ten cases the responsible minister rejected the criticism.

The cases can be classified as follows: abuse of position for personal benefit (23 cases); disregard of regulations, especially financial regulations for personal advantage (23 cases); conflict of interest (23 cases); suspected embezzlement or fraud (11 cases); improprieties in administration (4 cases); improprieties in tendering (3 cases); others (4 cases).

A look at the findings of this survey will show that some of the cases are characterized as being connected to a specific subject or specific entity, while others are characterized as 'horizontal' findings relating to the public service as a whole, or to significant sectors in the public service. Thus, for example, the state comptroller's findings regarding political appointments that were published in the state comptroller annual reports during Justice Ben-Porath's term of office led to legal and administrative amendments that affected major sectors of the public service in Israel. These amendments called for preventing and/or restricting political appointments in the government service, and arranging special processes for appointing directors to government corporations.[11]

Although the approach of the state comptroller to the issue of political appointments in the public service was criticized by, among others, scholars,[12] it should be mentioned that the High Court has recently referred to the issue, totally supporting the state comptroller's approach:

> The political appointment is a breach of trust of the executive branch against the public. It can influence the public's confidence in the

public service; it influences the equality of rights; it influences the professional standards of public officials, who are not demanded to prove, by tender, that they are the best. It can bring about a phenomenon characterized by preferring connections to qualifications; and politics in its narrow meaning turns out to be the major factor in the appointment. It can lead to the false organizing of a system, enabling the absorption of close political 'relatives' to speed up their advancement and to create unneeded jobs. It can corrupt the public moral integrity, unbalancing the stability and decreasing professionalism. It can harm the public servant's morale, influence the quality of the public service and hurt its image. In conclusion, the political appointment harms the basic principles of our judiciary system, our concept of values, our understanding of the essence of public service and of the social covenant, which is without a doubt the basis of our existence as human society.[13]

'TWILIGHT' TREATMENT IN A 'TWILIGHT' DOMAIN

Despite the prominent duty of the state comptroller to report infringements on moral integrity in his annual report,[14] it seems that this 'foggy' domain receives 'foggy' treatment. The state comptroller does not furnish the public with sufficient data on the efficiency of his follow-up and the outcomes of his findings and recommendations on issues of moral integrity – in spite of its importance to public opinion on this sensitive topic. By the same token, the state comptroller does submit, from time to time, matters suspected of being criminal acts that were included in his reports to the attorney general, in accordance with paragraph 14(c) of the State Comptroller Law. The attorney general has to examine the matter and, if he sees fit, to open the necessary procedures. Until 1996, no information was made public on these matters, not in the state comptroller's reports and not in any other way. In response to this criticism, the Knesset saw fit, in 1996, to amend the State Comptroller Law, adding to paragraph 14(c), 'The Attorney General will notify the State Comptroller and the Committee, within six months, as to how he handled the matter.'

Nevertheless, it should be emphasized again that there is no doubt that the state comptroller, his findings and his recommendations regarding issues of moral integrity and ethics in the public service have significant influence on the infrastructure of public service ethics in Israel. This is especially true in terms of conflict of interest dilemmas in the public service, receipt of benefits by state officials, preferences granted in various domains, prohibitions and limitations on extra jobs, limitations on 'revolving door' phenomena, limitations and restrictions on using information, etc. Another important contribution of the state comptroller is that of raising across the board issues of public service ethics. An interesting example is the state comptroller's report on grants allocated to institutions through local authorities (1991). In this report, the state comptroller uncovered the rooted procedures that were involved in these inappropriate acts. According to the state comptroller's opinion:

> The findings revealed during the examination indicate that the Ministry of the Interior did not inspect the activities of the local authorities concerning this matter, and did not prevent the deviations raised by the audit several times in the past. On the contrary, the ministry and its heads, who were supposed to supervise the implementation of the grants allocation procedure by the local authorities and their financial management, turned out to be the leaders of the unfit system of transferring grants to institutions without control nor criteria. Therefore, the norms binding every regular government, and the basic goal of the grants allocation procedure, which is to allocate grants based on equal criteria, were ignored. The damage that was caused to the government system was not merely financial damage that could be quantified. There was more than this; people got used to the idea that organizations and authorities can forward their interests even if it is against the law and orderly management.[15]

It seems that the boundaries of state audit examinations, in light of the moral integrity audit standard, can and are changing due to modifications in the social, political and public climate. The awareness of the state comptrollers to these changes and to the risks involved is vital, despite the political problems and complexities that could arise, and despite the unbridled attacks against the state audit institution and its head. This was the case when the state comptroller published his report on grants allocated to institutions through the local authorities.[16] Respected members, and even religious personalities, of the Shas party (the ultra-Orthodox Sephardi party) rudely attacked the then state comptroller, Justice Ben-Porath.[17]

MORAL INTEGRITY ISSUES IN THE MARGINS OF THE ISRAELI PUBLIC ADMINISTRATION

Geist and Friedberg suggest that the standards of observing moral integrity and public service ethics of the public administration system in Israel, and probably in other countries as well, are more flexible at the margins of the system than at the core.[18] In Israel, this domain includes a wide variety of entities, such as local governments, public corporations, organizations subsidized by the government, universities, the Jewish Agency, the

Histadrut (Labour Federation) and many other entities. In 1986, the state comptroller noted in his report on local government that, 'A considerable amount of the employee benefits in local government have been instituted since fiscal year 1982, i.e., after this was specifically forbidden by budget laws. It is reasonable to assume that much of this wholesale and blatant violation of the law could have been prevented if the Ministry of Interior, charged with supervising local government, had intervened in time.'[19]

There were serious findings in the state comptroller's 1995 report concerning the use of local authorities' budgets by mayors to finance personal or party election propaganda. The state comptroller noted that:

> This way, they unlawfully utilized the public purse for their personal benefit – beyond the sums allocated by law to the party they are members of – for this goal. Since we are facing a severe repeat occurrence, that was raised a number of times in the State Comptroller's reports, it is important to take steps without delay to uproot misuse, which is considered a severe transgression of moral integrity. As mentioned before, the approach of forgiveness only encourages the repetition of such acts, given that the sinners have nothing to be afraid of, and much to utilize. The use of public budgets for their goals enables them to increase their prospects for reelection and to accumulate political power; and if they are caught, at most they will be asked to return the money that they used anyway without authority and permission. This example illustrates other occurrences in public administration that exist and are well established for the same reason – there is no fear that public servants will be accountable for their misdeeds, despite their severity and the existence of legal directives that could be used against them. The law is designated not only for the simple citizen, but first and foremost for the powerful officials that should be an example and model for the public as his trustees.[20]

It should be noted that significant segments of the public sector in Israel are not audited by the state comptroller, but by other public auditors. They include the comptrollers of the Histadrut, of the Jewish Agency and of the World Zionist Organization. These comptrollers act within voluntary organizations. Their activities are based on a voluntary constitution in the Histadrut and on voluntary statutes in the Jewish Agency and the World Zionist Organization. The reports of the Histadrut and the Jewish Agency comptrollers show that standards of moral integrity and norms of ethics in these organizations are even more 'flexible'.

Comparing the approaches of these comptrollers to the approach of the state comptroller will show that there is an essential difference between them. For example, although the state comptroller has dealt repeatedly in the last decade with the serious issue of political appointments, it seems that this is a non-issue for the Histadrut and the Jewish Agency comptrollers. There are almost no findings in their reports concerning political appointments. It would not be a mistake to assume that this phenomenon is rooted deeply in these organizations.

In connection with this it should be noted that already in 1958, the Committee for Analysing Principles and Standards of Conduct of Public Officials saw fit to include in its recommendations not only the government sector but the entire public sector as well. This intention did not come to fruition. The reason was possibly to prevent the formation of different standards for the conduct of officials in the public sector. The risks involved in situations like this are clear: chances are that blurring and flexible processes will form different norms of ethics in various sub-sectors of the public sector – that which is forbidden in one sub-sector might become likely in another.

INTERNAL AUDITING AND MORAL INTEGRITY

A survey of the web of laws, regulations, directives, standards, etc. related to internal audit activities in Israel will show that examination of moral integrity in the Israeli public service is one of the internal auditor's duties as well. Paragraph 4(a) of the Internal Audit Law, 5752-1992 states, 'The internal auditor shall examine, inter alia, (1) if the activities of the public body in which he serves as auditor, and of the office holders and functionaries of that body, are in order with respect to due regard for the law, orderly administration, moral standards and economy and efficiency, and if they are effective in achieving the ends set for them.' In reference to the audit duties, it should be mentioned that the public and internal audit functions in Israel were inspired by the State Comptroller Law. Thus, for example, since the mid-1960s, the Civil Service Statutes, Chapter 65, detail the duties of the internal auditor in the government ministry, including his duty to examine moral integrity in his ministry. In this instance, the dependence factor of the internal audit function in comparison to the independence factor of the public audit function (the state comptroller for example) must be mentioned. It is interesting that phenomena defined clearly by the state comptroller and the judiciary as infringements on moral integrity are almost ignored, not only by public audit institutions in sectors that are not audited by the state comptroller, but also by internal auditors acting in accordance with the Internal Audit Law in government ministries, state authorities, government corporations, etc. that are audited by the state comptroller.[21]

Based on these findings, it seems that the questions of whose ethics and what ethics could be answered differently based on the location of sectors and entities in the margins of the public sector, far from the core government. Apparently, the audit activity concerning moral integrity will diminish as the audit institutions and functions become weaker.

ETHICAL ASPECTS INVOLVED IN THE ACTIVITIES OF THE STATE AUDIT INSTITUTION

The ethical aspects involved in the activities of the state audit institution itself comprise another important issue. It is interesting that the research dedicated to the issue is negligible. In this paper, I would like to mention a few points concerning the issue:

(1) The audit reports are final; there is no appeal. An entity, and even a person, could be harmed severely because of an audit report. It seems that in the State Comptroller Law, no attention was paid to remedies necessary for solving such problems. A good example is the Shachal–Terner case, in which the then state comptroller Justice Ben-Porath determined that Terner lied. This left Terner with no choice other than to appeal to the High Court.[22] The High Court ruled that, owing to judicial reasons, 'The consequences of the opinion are not valid.'[23]

(2) The state comptroller usually refers in his reports to entities and not to people. In the last few years, the state comptroller has increasingly mentioned in his reports names of office holders in the audited bodies, as well as elected public officials. The state comptroller even mentions names of people who do not belong to audited entities, for example, names of big donors to political parties, some of whom donate to more than one party.[24] No doubt that publishing names in audit reports raises many complicated ethical problems.

(3) Another issue has to do with the 'organizational example' that should be set by an institution like the State Comptroller's Office. The essence of the concept 'organizational example' is expressed by the assumption that an organization that 'preaches' efficiency, economy, change and improvement must – first and foremost – apply it within its own home. The state comptroller recommended, after a thorough examination, a series of activities to advance and improve internal auditing in the public service. There is a hitch, however. The state comptroller himself did not see fit to apply these recommendations to his own office. Until today, no internal audit unit functions in the State Comptroller's Office.

SOME CONCLUDING REMARKS

An examination of the state comptroller's reports, and reports of other public comptrollers, internal auditors in government ministries, government corporations, internal auditors in local authorities and other audit bodies, leads to the conclusion that there are several categories of moral integrity infringements with which most of the mentioned audit bodies will tend to deal. Namely, the more the infringements on moral integrity relate to deviations from orderly management and financial procedures, the more likely it is that audit bodies will tend to deal with them. These are mainly occurrences that are 'infected' by conflict of interests; use of outfits and items for private purposes; ignoring rules and directives, especially in the financial domain, for personal gain; irregular activities concerning tenders, etc.[25] It seems that the larger part of the administrative system is willing to accept that the audit bodies – public and internal – will handle such categories of infringements as required by law, directives, standards, etc. On the other hand, the more the infringements on moral integrity touch upon political issues, the more the audit will lessen, diminish, fade and even disappear. The diminishing and disappearing factors have two aspects:

(1) The further the entities and sectors are from the core government, located at the margins and the far-reaching margins, the less likely it is that public and internal audit activities will be carried out, especially moral integrity audits. Thus, for example, the state comptroller referred to political appointments at the margins of the administrative system, in the local authorities, for the first time in 1998, despite the fact that he began auditing this matter in the core government – government ministries and agencies – ten years earlier.[26]
(2) Internal audit units do not tend to deal with moral integrity issues that are connected, one way or another, to political matters. For example, the state comptroller dealt with the use of budgets of local authorities for financing election propaganda of mayors in several cities.[27] Although it is logical to assume that internal auditors in these local authorities were aware of this phenomenon, there is almost no mention in their reports of it.

There is no unequivocal consensus concerning what is considered an infringement on moral integrity – sometimes because of unclear norms and sometimes because norms simply do not exist at all. Nevertheless, it is widely accepted that the state comptroller is the commentator on moral integrity in the public service sector. This role has become a substantive feature of public and internal auditing in Israel.

Repeated infringements on moral integrity uncovered by the state comptroller point to the acceptance of negative normative phenomena by extensive populations in Israeli society (negative norms become normative). Some events that were unveiled could be defined as informal rights given to selected groups in public organizations and institutions. As Dr Nebenzhal, the late state comptroller, noted, 'We frequently encounter a conflict of norms. There are moral norms accepted by society as a whole and there are others particular to certain groups, in the broad sense of the term "group", i.e., a certain shared viewpoint of common interests. These groups often maintain that what is good for the group is good for society as a whole ... This perception is very dangerous. It frequently happens that a person begins by acting for the good of the group, but later, due to the habit of disregarding the demands of society as a whole, he acts for his own good.'

Infringements on moral integrity occur particularly in the 'normative hollows', 'twilight zones' of the public administration system. This is understandable, owing to the size, scope and high level of involvement of this system in the gamut of state activities and the extensiveness of contact points between citizens and public authorities.

The contributions of public and internal audit functions to the improvement of moral integrity and public service ethics can be found in the definitions of events as infringements on moral integrity, the wide acceptance of these definitions and the advancement of legislation and standardization in this 'foggy' area. In my report submitted to the Public–Professional Committee for the Thorough Examination of the Government Service (the Kubersky Committee, 1989), I emphasized that forming and implementing norms of behaviour in the public service are, first and foremost, the outcome of projecting authority and personal example, especially among high-ranking elected officials. 'The face of the administration is the face of its elected and high-ranking officials.'

In conclusion, many reasons – such as lack of charismatic authority, edicts that public service cannot keep, 'foggy' or non-existent norms, low salaries, and ill-conceived short-term solutions – have combined to create informal and unwritten rules of behaviour alongside the formal rules. The state and its agencies and authorities did not consider the dangers of these negative norms in time, these 'weeds' that sprouted in the 'garden' of public administration. In the medium and long term, the damage caused to public administration and society in Israel is not worth the short-term savings or profit, real or imagined, budgetary or other. It is difficult to maintain proper norms of behaviour in the daily running of public administration if the constituted authorities turn a blind eye, or sometimes even covertly welcome negative phenomena that stand in contradiction to the law and to moral behaviour. This is the plight of the Israeli public administration system. Without a doubt, it will be difficult to cut back this wild growth, but it is essential to begin. It seems that the definition of certain phenomena by the state comptroller as negative phenomena and infringements on moral integrity is an important phase, and a major contribution of the state comptroller to this difficult task.

NOTES

1. B. Geist and A. Friedberg, 'State Audit and Moral Integrity in the Government Service', *Studies in State Audit*, Vol. 53 (1995), pp.34–49 (in Hebrew).
2. I.E. Nebenzhal, 'The Meaning of "Moral Integrity" in the State Comptroller Law', in N. Lipshitz, I. Ganon and R. Hecht (eds.), *Abraham Weinshall, Publications in His Memory*, Haifa: Shikmona, 1977 (in Hebrew).
3. E.M. Wheat, 'The Activist Auditor: A New Player in State and Local Politics', *Public Administration Review*, Vol. 51, No. 5 (Sept./Oct. 1991), pp.385–92.
4. Nebenzhal, 'The Meaning of "Moral Integrity" in the State Comptroller Law'.
5. J. Maltz, 'State Audit, Goals and Directions', in A. Friedberg (ed.), *State Audit, Knesset and Government*, Jerusalem: The Civil Service Commission, Central School of Administration, 1988, pp.23–40 (in Hebrew).
6. Criminal Appeal 884/80, *The State of Israel v. Grossman*, Piskei Din (Judgments) XXXVI(1), 405–22 (in Hebrew).
7. I. Sharkansky, 'Too Much of the Wrong Things', *The Jerusalem Quarterly*, Vol. 45 (Winter 1988), pp.1–26.
8. State Comptroller's Office, *Report on Audit of the Local Government Sector*, Jerusalem: State Comptroller's Office, 1998 (in Hebrew).
9. State Comptroller's Office, *Report on the Appointment of Directors in Government Corporations*, Jerusalem: State Comptroller's Office, 1989 (in Hebrew).
10. Geist and Friedberg, 'State Audit and Moral Integrity in the Government Service'.
11. See State Comptroller's Office, *Annual Reports* 39, 1989; 41, 1991; 43, 1993; 44, 1994; 45, 1995; 47, 1997; 48, 1998; *Report on Appointment of Directors in Government Corporations*, 1989; *Report on Audit of Local Government*, 1998 (all published in Jerusalem: State Comptroller's Office).
12. D. Dery, *Political Appointments in Israel*, Jerusalem: The Israel Democracy Institute, 1983 (in Hebrew).
13. High Court of Justice 145/98, *The New Labour Federation and the Federation of Academics in Social Sciences and Humanities v. The State of Israel, the Minister of Construction and Housing and Shimon Einstein, Director of the Department for Rural Building*, 1998, para. 10 (in Hebrew).
14. Paragraph 15(b)(1) of the State Comptroller Law.
15. State Comptroller's Office, *Report on the Audit of Allocating Grants to Institutions Through Local Authorities*, Jerusalem, 1991, p.24 (in Hebrew).
16. Ibid.
17. *Globes*, 24 July 1991.
18. Geist and Friedberg, 'State Audit and Moral Integrity in the Government Service'.
19. State Comptroller's Office, *Report on Audit of the Local Government Sector*, Jerusalem: State Comptroller's Office, 1986.
20. State Comptroller's Office, *Report on Audit of the Local Government Sector*, Jerusalem: State Comptroller's Office, 1995.
21. For a detailed analysis encompassing the ethical issues involved in internal auditing activities, see A. Friedberg, 'Ethical Aspects of Internal Auditing', *Journal of Business Ethics*, Vol. 17 (1998), pp. 895–904.
22. State Comptroller's Office, *Opinion on the Chain of Events that Brought about the Resignation of Inspector General Jacob Terner*, Jerusalem: State Comptroller's Office, 1994.
23. High Court of Justice 4914/94, *Jacob Terner v. The State Comptroller and the Knesset Committee for State Auditing*, 1995 (in Hebrew).
24. State Comptroller's Office, *Annual Report 41*, Jerusalem: State Comptroller's Office, 1991.
25. Geist and Friedberg, 'State Audit and Moral Integrity in the Government Service'.
26. State Comptroller's Office, *Report on the Audit of the Local Government Sector*, Jerusalem: State Comptroller's Office, 1998.
27. State Comptroller's Office, *Report on the Audit of the Local Government Sector*, Jerusalem: State Comptroller's Office, 1995.

Abstracts

Introduction
Moshe Maor

This article poses two central questions faced by Israeli political executives nowadays. Are bureaucratic structures the problem or the solution? Are civil servants the problem or the solution? It tries to estimate the direction of developments in the Israeli administrative system and the derived consequence in terms of the answers to these questions. The article argues that it is reasonable to expect, as always in the Israeli context, that different parts of the administrative system are most likely to move in different directions. Some ministerial departments may remain under the ambit of the Weberian model, others may follow the New Public Management model, and others may be moving towards a mix of mechanisms used according to circumstances. Another argument advanced here is that factors which may inhibit reforms include a weakness of mechanisms for policy control, monitoring and evaluation; and an administrative culture which is characterized by frequent infringements of moral integrity and a relatively high level of politicization. The latter is probably the problem that the success of any reform is dependent on and will be judged upon.

The Development of the Israeli Government Offices
Aharon Kfir

Israel's civil service, in general, and the structure of its government offices, in particular, have been fraught with problems ever since the state was established. This article examines the process which led to the creation of government offices from 1943 to 1948. Based on historical and institutional analysis, it shows that a great deal of thought was given to the structure of the government service. The outcome was a well-founded structure for government offices, well able to stand the test of modern administrative challenges. The distortions in the execution of this plan stemmed, and still stem, in the main, from non-compliance with the detailed original plans owing, mainly, to political considerations. Since the establishment of the state there has been continuous criticism of the structure of government administration and there have been numerous proposals for change. Almost every one of these proposals was aimed at the elimination of three main shortcomings: curtailment of the number of

government offices; reorganization of the functions of the various offices
in order to maximize coordination; and development of directional
planning and coordinated supervision of activities – the need for which
the earlier planning had tried to obviate in its proposals.

Administrative Power in Israel
Eva Etzioni-Halevy

The power of the state administration in Israel is considerable but not
autonomous. Rather, the administrative elite is dependent on the political
elite through political appointments and promotions in some major parts of
the state bureaucracy. By virtue of this close but unequal connection,
administrative power is linked to party politics and works in its service:
senior bureaucrats have been instrumental in various forms of electoral
manipulation. Over the years there have been changes and developments,
but there has been no fundamental transformation of these arrangements.
This creates severe problems for Israeli democracy. The electoral
manipulation brought about by administrative politicization has not
destroyed democracy. But it has not been negligible in determining electoral
outcomes. Hence it has detracted from the quality of democracy in Israel.

The Functioning of Whatever Is the Israeli State
Ira Sharkansky

Distinctive features of Israeli public administration reflect underlying
traits of the nation's history, culture and geography. The concentration of
people in part of the small state produces a dominant metropolitan region.
The formal structure and procedures are those of a strong national
government, and there is a high incidence of former technocrats in elected
positions. The image is of a tightly run, professional state. However, the
formal structure provides imperfect indications of how policy-making and
programme implementation really operate. Other features of the political
culture, along with the high incidence of intense problems, create a messy
polity where coping rather than problem-solving prevails.

Controlling Government: Budgeting, Evaluation and Auditing in Israel
Robert Schwartz

Is Israel's government out of control? This article provides a snapshot of
the state of administrative and financial control of government activities
in Israel. Budgeting, evaluation and auditing mechanisms are examined in

the light of changes in international approaches and practice – post-bureaucratic control and the advent of the 'audit society'. There is no lack of control mechanisms, including a plethora of audit functions, but their implementation is weak. Bureaucratic procedural compliance dominates both budgeting and auditing practice at the expense of post-bureaucratic, results-based control. There is little parliamentary supervision. And budgeting, auditing and evaluation activities are weakly linked. Explanations of the sorry state of administrative control in Israel include: agenda overload; highly politicized coalition-type government; and a cultural tendency of lack of thoroughness.

Judicial Accountability in Israel: The High Court of Justice and the Phenomenon of Judicial Hyperactivism
Yoav Dotan

This article describes the general characteristics of the judicial system in Israel and its relationship with other institutions in Israeli society. It presents a model of society within which the courts (and, in particular, the Supreme Court) play a paramount political role by routinely intervening in the practices of the public administration as well as in the business of other governmental and non-governmental institutions, and thereby bringing about a judicialization of society. The courts intervene in decision-making processes of other institutions, and this widespread intervention brings about a process of adaptation to patterns of legal thinking and judicial decision-making by many other administrative institutions. I will call this model of highly intensive judicial intervention 'judicial hyperactivism'.

Choosing a Regulatory Regime: The Experience of the Israeli Electricity Market
Moshe Maor

If there is a choice of institutional designs for the regulation of public utilities, how can such a choice be made between, for example, a single- or a multiple-industry regulator? This question is addressed in this paper by focusing on the design of the Israeli Public Utility Authority – Electricity, with special attention to the ways it has interpreted the requirements set by law regarding accountability, transparency and procedural fairness. The premise underlying the analysis is that regulators need to satisfy values of accountability, transparency and procedural fairness if they are to receive the approval of all parties concerned. A failure to implement choices that reflect these values implies that, whatever the substantive merits of such decisions, the subsequent regulation is unlikely to be successful. Based on institutional and historical analysis, combined with interviews with public officials involved with the design of the electricity regulator, the paper analyses the formation of the Public Utility Authority with an emphasis on the prominence, or the lack thereof, of the aforementioned values in the Electricity Market Law 1996 and the Authority's experience gained so far. The analysis finds that a lack of balance exists between the great discretion enjoyed by the Authority over tariffs and standard-setting, on the one hand, and its weak transparency, accountability and procedural fairness, on the other. The paper recommends an urgent revision of the law. In addition, to avoid creating other regulatory agencies that will suffer from similar structural and procedural flaws, the paper recommends the design of accountable, transparent and procedurally fair, single-industry regulators.

The Role of State and Public Audit in Safeguarding Ethics in the Public Service: Whose Ethics? What Ethics?
Asher Friedberg

This article discusses the role of state and public audit entities in Israel in safeguarding ethics in the public service. It relates to ambiguities and complexities concerning the legal and content infrastructure in the light of which the state comptroller examines ethical issues in the public service sector, and refers to approaches of state comptrollers, past and present, to ethical issues in this sector. The article analyses a series of events and findings that were defined by state comptrollers as infringements of moral integrity, trying to identify patterns of infringements and to trace actions taken to remedy these infringements. The article mentions activities of other public comptrollers (the Labour Federation and the Jewish Agency) to moral integrity issues. It points to ethical aspects in the activities of the State Comptroller's Office itself, and concludes by emphasizing problems stemming from the discussion in the article.

Index

accommodation, 56, 57, 62
Accountant General's Division, 72
accountability, 3, 6–7, 70, 80, 82, 108, 116–18, 137–8; programme accountability, 74
administration, 1, 2, 6, 29, 58, 82; administrative action, 28, 88–9, 102; advanced administration techniques, 9; agency, 90, 109; authority, 96; culture, 4, 76, 135; elite 5, 25–8, 37, 136; innovation, 10; institution, 88, 137; politicization, 5, 50; position, 50, 52; power, 5, 25–8, 36–9, 42–3, 136; reforms, 1, 25, 67; regulation, 16; requirement, 19; rule, 52; system, 122, 125, 132–3, 135; unit, 72
ageing, 75
agenda, 6, 46, 59–60, 82, 94, 97, 99, 100, 137
agreement, 68; disagreement, 59
agriculture quotas, 90
allocation, 66
ambiguity, 56–7, 58–9, 62, 121–2; ambiguity of politics, 57
American Jewish Joint Distribution Committee, 74–5
American National Performance Review, 71
analysis, 73; cost-benefit analysis, 73; analysis techniques, 73
appointment, 11, 27–8, 29, 32, 38–9, 50, 51, 109, 127; personnel, 54; political, 1, 5, 14, 27–9, 31–2, 37–8, 40, 42, 50, 82, 123–7, 130, 132, 136; procedures, 32
Arafat, Y., 58–9
Arian, A., 77
Aron, R., 25
Asia, 59
Assembly of Representation, 11
assignment of position, 19
association, 56, 70
Arab association, 56
Arab, 13, 54, 55, 56, 57, 89
Attorney General, 91–2, 93, 94, 99, 127
audit, 69–70, 77–8, 122, 124–5, 128, 131–2; body, 121, 124, 131–2; external audit, 71; financial audit, 68; formal audit, 66; function, 5; institution, 131; internal audit, 71, 79, 80–81, 130–33; society, 6, 66, 77, 80, 83, 137; standard, 121, 128; National Audit Office, 66, 68, 78; post-bureaucratic mode audit, 80; public audit, 132–3, 138; public audit institution, 130, 138; report, 131; resource, 77, 81; state audit, 81, 121,
125, 126; state audit institution, 7, 66, 79, 124–5, 128, 131; Supreme Audit Institutions (SAIs), 76, 78
Audit Commission 66
auditing, 6, 66, 72, 76, 79–82, 124, 132, 137; mechanism, 82, 136; state auditing, 81, 124; system, 83; value-for-money auditing, 65
auditor, 66, 79, 124, 129; internal auditor, 80–81, 131–2; external state auditor, 80; public auditor, 130; state auditor, 80
Australia, 28, 78
Authority, 56, 57, 58, 61, 89, 125; with judicial power, 90
autonomy of the court system, 93
autonomous governmental unit, 65

Balfour Declaration, 11
Barak, A., 95–6
Barak, E., 50
Bar-Am, U., 35
Belgium, 28, 46
benefit, 55, 62, 108
Ben-Gurion, D., 9, 12, 15, 17–19
Ben Porat, M., 54–5, 123, 125–6, 128, 131
Benstein, P., 18–20
Ben-Tov, M., 18
Besanko, D., 109
bill of rights, 88–9; 'unwritten bill of rights', 90
Britain, 13, 28, 78, 91; Colonial Office, 12; government, 11; House of Commons, 68; House of Lords, 99; law, 15; mandate, 88; model of reforms, 2
Brookdale Institute, 74–6
Brovender, S., 114
Buchart, Ross E., 27
budget, 15, 66–73, 77; allocation, 70; division, 67; implementation report, 69; spending, 70; system, 67
Budget Law of 1985, 19, 68
budgeting, 6, 66–73, 82–3, 129, 136–7; analysis-based budgeting, 73; budgeting process, 73
bureaucracy, 1–4, 79, 88, 93, 97, 99, 101, 102; bureaucracy-bashing, 1; bureaucrat, 53, 109; bureaucratic elite, 36; bureaucratic model, 76–7, 79; bureaucratic-hierarchic model, 66, 67; bureaucratic procedures, 3, 6, 81, 82; bureaucratic structures, 1, 135; bureaucratic-style operation, 110;

For Product Safety Concerns and Information please contact our EU
representative GPSR@taylorandfrancis.com Taylor & Francis Verlag GmbH,
Kaufingerstraße 24, 80331 München, Germany

Printed and bound by CPI Group (UK) Ltd, Croydon, CR0 4YY
10/06/2025
01898340-0002